5 Kids on Wild Trails: A Memoir

Margaret Fuller

Elephant's Perch (The Saddleback) in the Sawtooth Wilderness, Idaho.

Leslie in the Hikeapoose at Grass Lake near Fallen Leaf, California, 1961. (photo by Wayne Fuller)

TRAIL GUIDE BOOKS

Published by
Trail Guide Books
P.O. Box 148
Weiser, Idaho 83672

Manufactured in the United States

Cover and book design by Matt TeNgaio of Trail Guide Books

All photographs by the author unless otherwise noted

Cover photograph: The Fuller children in the Bighorn Crags.

Fuller, Margaret, 1935–

ISBN 978-0-9911561-5-3

5 Kids on Wild Trails: A Memoir

Margaret Fuller

TRAIL GUIDE BOOKS

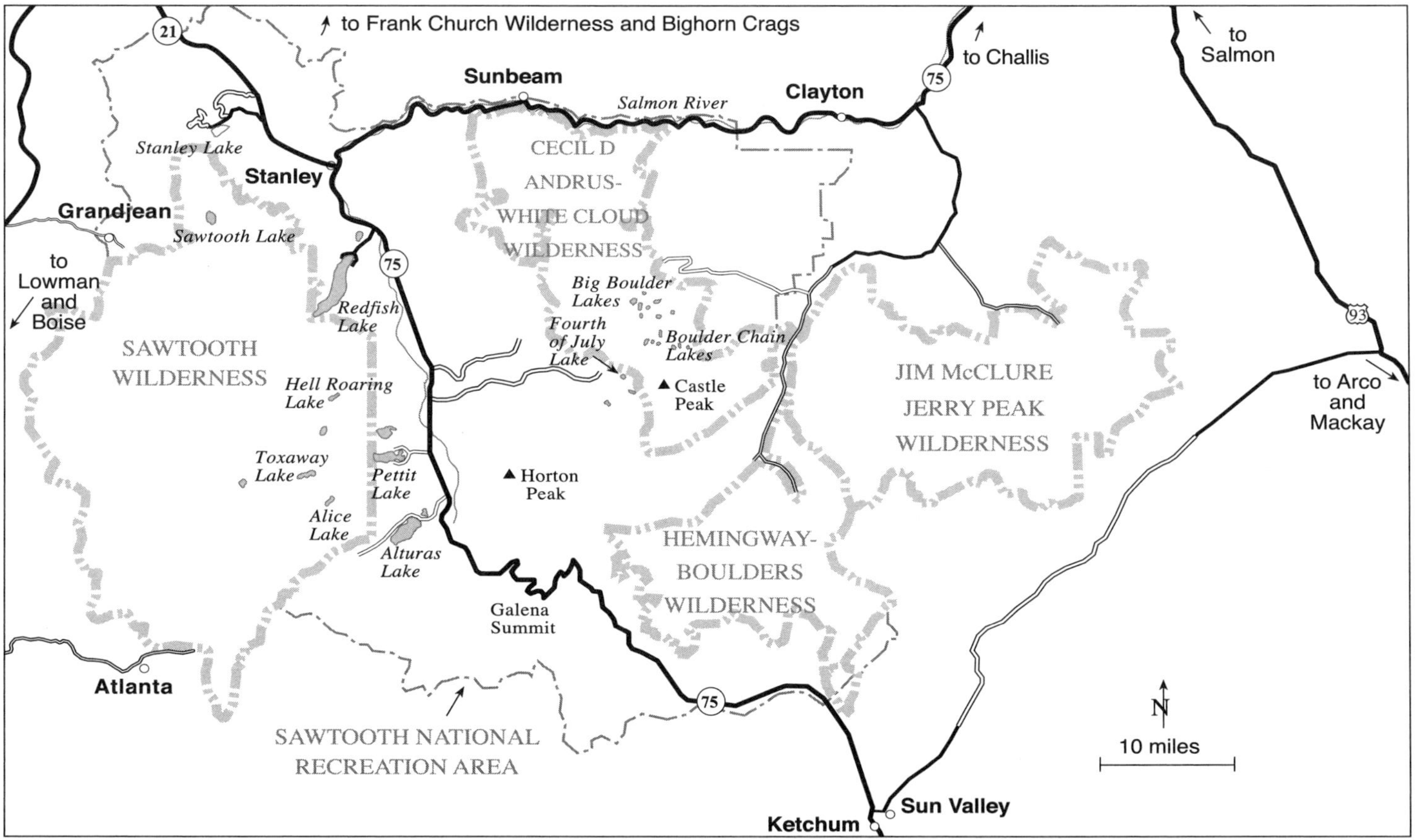
to Frank Church Wilderness and Bighorn Crags
21
to Challis
75
to Salmon
Sunbeam
Salmon River
Clayton
Stanley Lake
Stanley
CECIL D
ANDRUS-
WHITE CLOUD
WILDERNESS
Grandjean
Sawtooth Lake
to Lowman and Boise
Redfish Lake
Big Boulder Lakes
Fourth of July Lake
Boulder Chain Lakes
Castle Peak
93
SAWTOOTH
WILDERNESS
Hell Roaring Lake
JIM McCLURE
JERRY PEAK
WILDERNESS
to Arco and Mackay
Toxaway Lake
Pettit Lake
Horton Peak
Alice Lake
Alturas Lake
HEMINGWAY-
BOULDERS
WILDERNESS
Galena Summit
Atlanta
SAWTOOTH NATIONAL
RECREATION AREA
N
10 miles
Sun Valley
Ketchum

5 KIDS ON WILD TRAILS: A MEMOIR

TABLE OF CONTENTS

The five kids on wrong track while trying to find 4th of July Lake in 1969.

CHAPTER 1: THE ONLY MAP WAS BEAR VALLEY 1896

Two summers ago the road up 4th of July Creek in the White Clouds was a gravel Forest Service road. It no longer had the boulders and tire-swallowing ruts of my first trip up this road in 1969. To us 4th of July Lake was very beautiful. My husband Wayne and I planned to hike to 4th of July Lake under the fluted cliffs of Patterson Peak. I have been in love with mountains ever since I can remember. In this story I attempt to trace what that has led me to do.

When I had tried to take my five young children to Fourth of July Lake in 1969, without Wayne, we had hiked up a jeep road instead of a trail and not found any lake. That experience changed my life.

The 2018 hike I figured would be my 40th to this lake, if I counted passing it on the way to other places. We had tried to go to 4th of July in 2017 but forty feet of knee deep water over mud had blocked the road about five miles up it. The high runoff had come from the deep snow winter of 2016-17, snow so deep that the roof of our only grocery store in Weiser where we live had fallen in. The chief trail ranger, Jay Dorr, told me it had taken 38 truckloads of rock to fill the hole in the 4th of July Road.

I parked our Explorer under lodgepole pines in the parking lot. Then Wayne and I started out with our day packs and trekking poles. Wayne wore his Tilly hat, which covered his balding white hair. The hat was the kind that is guaranteed for life and he had already had it replaced once. As I tightened my boot laces, I remembered that on that first trip I had worn jeans and high-topped sneakers. Jeans and sneakers were what I had worn hiking in the Sierras when I was young. The parking lot, outhouse, horse-loading ramp and sign-in box were 200 yards before the meadow where I had thought the road ended in 1969. It had actually gone another half mile to a dusty slope beside a fallen-in log cabin. Then I had seen no other cars. Today we had to search to find a parking place.

When we had hiked to 4th of July Lake two years earlier with a friend, it had taken us a little over two hours. In 2018 I am ashamed to say it took me three hours. Although Wayne had a painful hip he could still walk much faster than I could. Now I am too afraid of falling to try to go fast even with trekking poles. But I still love hiking in the mountains and was just glad to be able to see the lake again. As I placed each foot and pole, trying not to trip, I wondered why not being able to find Fourth of July Lake so many years ago had such a big effect on me.

On that long-ago day I had taken the children into the white clapboard ranger station in Sawtooth Valley to ask the ranger, Ralph Cisco, what hikes would be good for my kids. Doug, Leslie, Neal, and Hilary clustered around the scarred oak desk. As I stood with two-year-old Stuart on one hip, one of his little red tennis shoes dug into my stomach. The smoke from the wood stove made me sneeze. It was a crisp day in mid-June. As the tanned and wiry ranger handed me a Forest Service map, he said, "Easiest hike for kids? Maybe Sawtooth Lake in the Sawtooths and Fourth of July Lake in the White Clouds. Sawtooth Lake is four miles, and Fourth of July Lake is only a mile."

He pointed out those lakes and their access roads on the map. The one mile hike sounded like the right size for the kids. "What is the road to the Fourth of July trailhead like?", I asked.

"What kind of a car do you have?"

"An International Travelall, but it doesn't have four-wheel drive."

"It has a high wheelbase, doesn't it? You should be able to make it all right. You won't need four-wheel drive."

Outside the station, I savored the smell of sagebrush and pine. Above the sagebrush-covered hills behind the ranger station rose some white peaks that looked as though they had been colored on the sky with chalk. I knew these peaks were part of the White Clouds. In the opposite direction across the meanders of the Salmon River, the Sawtooth Mountains resembled a giant crosscut saw set against a cobalt blue sky.

The Sawtooths had been a formal wilderness then for only five years, since the Wilderness Act was passed in 1964. They were still unspoiled except for a little trash and a few paths between trail switchbacks. By then, two subdivisions had brought power poles and an airstrip to the valley between the ranges. However the White Clouds were being threatened by a huge molybdenum mine thatt the American Smelting Mining and Refining Company had proposed.

In 1967 hearings had been held in Sun Valley on legislation to make the Sawtooths and White Clouds a National Recreation Area and the bill had been re-introduced that year. By the time of our first attempt to hike from our cabin into the White Clouds in 1969, it hadn't yet passed. From what I saw of the white peaks that 1969 day I thought the White Clouds should also be a wilderness.

That day we were hiking from our new cabin for the first time. Excitement fizzed within me at being in the mountains again. I had grown up hiking in the Sierras from my grandfather's cabin every summer. That had been the best part of the year for me. Once Wayne, Doug, and a carpenter had built the shell of our Sawtooth cabin the summer before, I couldn't wait to stay there and hike. Wayne wasn't with us that June day in 1969 because he was on a business trip to Pocatello.

Ten days earlier we had taken furniture to the cabin shell so we could begin to stay in it. The furniture included our old electric stove, four used army cots, four new cot mattresses, some old kitchen chairs, our old double mattress and springs, two plastic five gallon water containers, and a door we set on cinder blocks for a temporary table. Four year old Hilary had helped me wash dishes in a little creek 50 yards from the cabin. I cooked in an electric skillet plugged into an orange extension cord that led to an outlet on the power pole outside. Into a second extension cord I plugged Wayne's mother's old turkey roaster to heat water. When I wasn't heating water or cooking I plugged in a lamp that hung from a nail. Using Wayne's dad's old power saw I had constructed a box with a hole in it for a toilet seat. Wayne had set the box on a hole he dug in the woods and hung a tarp around the box. The cabin was finished and painted brown on the outside but inside it was just chipboard and two by fours. It stood in a Forest Service cabin area three miles up a rough dirt road from the highway between Sun Valley and Stanley. There were then seven or eight other cabins in it. From our cabin's sagebrush covered knoll we could see mountains peeking over timber ridges across the valley. Some were pink and gray and others resembled mounds of vanilla ice cream.

Before Wayne left for Pocatello I had told him I was thinking of taking the kids to the cabin while he was gone. He had said, "It's too dangerous to take them there by yourself. Why don't you wait until I can go too?"

"When can you go?"

"When I have my vacation at the end of July."

I looked at his tall rangy form with his shock of light brown hair and realized with a slight feeling of wickedness that I didn't have to do what he said. The end of July was six weeks away. I couldn't wait that long, besides I was tired of hearing Wayne's lawyer talk. "It's too dangerous. One of the children might break their leg and then what would you do? It is 40 miles to Ketchum where there are doctors and we don't have a phone. The only cabin that does is the Hunts and they won't be there yet. You might have a flat tire and you don't know how to change it and neither does Doug. One of the kids might wander off. And if you found someone to help you and they got hurt, they might sue us.

So the day before I had driven the kids to the cabin anyway.

Outside the ranger station, I loaded the kids into the car, and a few minutes later we were bouncing along over the baseball and football-sized rocks of the Fourth of July Creek Road. Alongside it, aspens and grasses glowed with the new green of spring. The air was thick with the smell of sagebrush. Ahead, wooded ridges hid the chalk-white summits I had seen from the ranger station. Far up the canyon a gray peak raised a wall of snow-filled chimneys.

Soon, the two-track road crossed the creek on a bridge. Here the water rushed along in big white curls. Arrowleaf balsamroot flowers splashed the hills with bright yellow. A small rabbit with black-tipped ears bounced across the road in front of us.

The ruts in the road became a foot deep, and the rocks grew to the size of cantaloupes and jack-o-lanterns. Adrenaline made the back of my neck prickle, but there was no place to turn around. I hadn't yet heard of the steep roads covered with boulders that one ranger calls Idaho freeways

I wanted my children to see these mountains up close, but it was really me who yearned to see them. If I could get to these mountains again, I would feel more connected to Idaho. I would have something like Fallen Leaf here. In Idaho women sewed, cooked, and canned, raised large families, and organized church bazaars. They usually limited their talk to those subjects or what people I had never heard of were doing. None of them took their children camping or hiking by themselves. I didn't think I would never fit in but I thought being close to its mountains would make me feel better.

We soon came to a 20-foot-long puddle that covered the road. I stopped the car. Doug, who was then 13, opened the car door, saying, "Let me see how deep it is."

He picked up a stick, stuck it into the puddle, and showed me the water line, "It's only about six inches deep and the bottom is sandy, not mud. Can't we go on?"

Ten-year-old Leslie said, "Turn around, Mom, we'll get stuck."

"We there yet? Get out?" asked Stuart, bouncing up and down.

The car made it through the water, but I began to feel sick to my stomach from fear.

Because my parents had introduced me to hiking as a child, I had fallen in love with the beauty of mountains. Thus I didn't feel it was odd to take my children hiking by myself, even 20 miles from the nearest civilization, which was the village

Stuart at Yellowbelly trailhead.

of Obsidian. It had so few people its population wasn't listed on the state map. My parents had taken me, my brother Tom and sister Dodie hiking from a trailhead called Glen Alpine Springs. It was three miles of boulders from the Fallen Leaf store, where the phone sometimes worked, and the store was 20 miles from the businesses at the south end of Lake Tahoe.

As I drove along the bumpy road, now and then I glanced at my children. Blonde, curly-haired Stuart stood next to me. He was attached to the front seat by a harness and a seat belt installed vertically. Holding his dirty white blanket to his face and sucking the middle fingers of one hand, he stared out at the road. Beside him sat Doug, who wore a jacket covered with ski patches. A fisherman's cap covered most of his dark gold hair. Black horn-rimmed glasses added to the worried look on his freckled face. Behind me, four-year-old Hilary kicked the seat as she sang made-up words to the tune of *Row, Row Your Boat*. When I glanced behind me to tell her to stop kicking, she scowled at me under the too-long bangs of her straight, dark blonde hair. Beside her, Leslie sang the right words, but Hilary said, "NO, don't sing. That's MY song." In the lulls in the singing, I could hear seven-year-old Neal humming from the way back as we called it, the cargo space at the back of the car. The tune sounded like *Dead Skunk in the Middle of the Road*, a song Neal knew I hated.

Leslie said, "He's singing that again. Make him stop."

I ignored her. Singing an annoying song wasn't as bad as some of the things he could be doing. "Mom," Leslie said, "you made me come to the cabin, and I'm missing swim practice. Elizabeth will beat me on Saturday. At least you can make Neal stop singing."

I stopped the car, shifted it into park, and turned around. "Neal, please sing something that is not Dead Skunk in the Middle of the Road."

His small freckled face peered over the back seat and smirked. "Ninety-nine bottles of beer on the wall", he began.

"Mom!" Leslie said, poking my shoulder and glaring at me.

"All right, everybody," I said, "Just be quiet! I have to pay attention to the road! if you don't want us to get stuck up here."

My children were so lovable and cute one moment, and so obnoxious the next.

Yet all of them had wanted to go on the hike when we left the cabin that morning. Neal had said, "We're going to get close to my white mountains, aren't we?" He had claimed them as his mountains because he had seen them first from the Alturas Lake beach.

The ruts soon deepened to trenches and it was hard to decide which to follow. The road couldn't get any worse, I thought, so I kept going.

After a tense half hour, the road forded a side stream in a little gully. When I drove into it and shifted into low gear, the engine died. Leslie cleared her throat and said, "I told you, you should have turned around."

I sighed, turned, and looked at her and Hilary in the back seat. Leslie folded her arms and scowled, her blonde curls hidden under a white sailor cap with its brim turned down. Hilary, wearing a pink cable knit sweater in spite of the warm day, peered out from under the too-long bangs of her short, straight hair. She asked, "Are we stuck, Mommy?"

"NO, we're not stuck," I said, shaking my head. "The engine just stopped a minute."

"Pull out the choke," called Neal from the back.

"If you do that, you'll flood it," said Doug.

I pulled the choke out a little, started the car, raised my foot from the clutch and drove through the stream. Ahead, watermelon-sized rocks covered a steep slope, but I kept going. The children kept quiet; probably they were as scared as I was. I sped up so the car wouldn't slide back. Now and then its underside thunked on a rock. Ahead I glimpsed a cocoa-colored mountain striped with snow. We made it up the slope of big rocks, only to face another stretch just like it. This road should have been closed a long time ago I thought, but if it had been, the trail would have been much longer than one mile.

After an hour of driving, we reached a meadow. Here the two ruts of the road forded a six foot wide side creek and disappeared. Above on the left, were piles of rock and jumbled sheets of rusty tin. Although there were no other cars here, I thought this creek must be the end of the road. When I pulled off the track and stopped, my fingers were numb. I drew in a big breath of the pine-scented air, smiled, and yawned. I was happy to be high in the mountains and tried not to think about the fact that Wayne had asked me not to take the kids to the cabin until he could go with us. I felt guilty and tired. I hadn't slept much the night before because I was afraid burglars or a bear would come in the night, and we had no phone to call for help. And I hadn't seen cars at any of the other cabins.

In the meadow, the grass glistened, dotted with yellow buttercups and magenta shooting stars. A jeep track went off to the right from the meadow across the main creek so I thought it was the trail. The chocolate-striped mountain overlooked the meadow. The beauty almost made up for the bad road.

Before the trip the only topographic map of the area I had been able to find was Bear Valley 1896. Now I got it out, but it didn't show any trails in the White Clouds so was no help. I had a Forest Service map as well, and it showed the trail to Fourth of July Lake going off to the right. There were no signs, but I thought the jeep track must be the trail or lead to it in a few yards.

I let the kids out of the car and we began to get ready for the hike. Doug put on my old army-surplus pack containing our peanut butter and jam sandwiches. Oranges, and cookies and two ponchos to make a shelter in case of rain. I put on my sunbonnet and the baby carrier we called the hikeapoose. It was a pack frame with a canvas bucket attached to it with cutouts for the child's legs. The frame lacked a waistband, so all the weight rested on my shoulders. However, it was a lot better than the little pack frame and three belts we had used to carry Doug to the Bench Lakes in the Sawtooths eleven years earlier. Doug corralled Stuart and stuffed him into the hikeapoose.

We started out on the jeep track, and within 100 yards, it forded knee-deep Fourth of July Creek. Doug, Leslie, and I waded across. On the other side, I took off the hikeapoose with Stuart in it and left them with Leslie. Then Doug and I waded back to get the other kids. Doug carried Hilary, and I helped Neal wade across. Beyond the creek, the jeep road didn't turn into a trail as I expected. There were still no signs and snowbanks began to cover the shady spots.

After about a mile, snow covered the whole road. Hilary plumped down in the snow, pulled off a red tennis shoe, and said, "Mommy, my feet are fweezing!"

Ahead I heard the thumps of snowballs, and Neal yelling, "Stop it. No fair!" Feeling annoyed it was so snowy, I wished I had bought Hilary the high-topped sneakers and the thick woolly socks the older kids and I wore. I hugged her, saying, "We'll get to the lake pretty soon and then you can take off your shoes and socks and play in the sand."

Hilary still found hiking difficult even without snow because she was born with her feet turned straight out. To straighten them, she had worn a foot brace day and night until she was 17 months old. Because of it she didn't learn to walk until then.

After another mile of walking through snow, the road split at a flattish rock outcrop. Beyond it, the snow on both roads deepened . All around us, meltwater dripped and trickled. The right-hand road aimed toward a pile of orange rock and a tunnel in a cliff, and the other road disappeared in trees straight ahead.

Neal pulled on the hikeapoose, tilting it, and asked, "Why did they put the lake so far?"

"Nobody put the lakes where they are. Glaciers carved them thousands of years ago," I replied, trying not to laugh. I took hold of his hands so he wouldn't pull me and Stuart over.

"Keep going! The lake's just a little farther," Doug called from the road ahead.

"What if it's not? Hilary and Neal are getting cold. We're going to have to go back. Let's eat lunch and talk about it."

I turned around and started back.

"Why do we have to turn around?" Neal asked.

"It's too snowy and we should have come to the lake by now if we're going the right way."

"Lunch now!" said Hilary. "Ow!" A snowball thrown by Neal hit her neck. "Mommy, make him stop it!"

I went back to the outcrop and sat down. Doug got out the lunch. We hadn't reached the lake, but at least we knew the way back to the car

When I let Stuart out of the hikeapoose, I was afraid he'd fall off the edge of the road, for the hillside plunged into the canyon below it. A picture of the kids sitting on the rock, shows them all scowling, except for Stuart, who didn't understand what was going on. Hilary kept her eyes shut, maybe pretending she was somewhere else.

Later I would laugh about this first one of the many wild goose chases I took my family on, but that day I was angry at the ranger, the Forest Service, and myself for choosing the wrong hike.

Back in Caldwell the next day, Wayne returned from his business trip while the kids and I were still unpacking. He walked up to me, carrying his briefcase in one hand and a red and brown-striped tie in the other. Strands of his hair stood up in the heat, and his sloping forehead shone with sweat. A grim expression erased his usual crooked smile. He said, "I'm very disappointed you didn't pay any attention to what I said about going to the cabin."

He stomped upstairs to change his clothes. What did I expect? He had given up Army Reserve and its summer camp that he enjoyed and spent his whole vacation the summer before building the cabin. I had ignored the many dangers in June, and the fact that the cabin had no phone.

In mountaineering and natural history books, the authors never question the importance of mountain expeditions. They rarely say anything about the people they leave at home, like John Muir's wife and daughters. I had been raised on hiking adventures. Even today it is hard for me to realize there are people who don't even like mountains let alone want to hike in them. I knew that Wayne loved mountains, too, but he loved the law and working in that field as much, and politics even more. For me, mountains were the most important thing besides family.

Later that first summer of the cabin, Wayne said I could take the kids up there a week before his vacation started. I was still determined to find a hike that worked. With the kids I walked down to see some neighbors named Hunt, who were teachers from Elko. They and their boys had befriended Wayne and Doug when they were building the cabin the summer before. Charlene suggested we try the shortcut to Hell Roaring Lake that they had once taken. It was only two miles and the trail was level. She had rheumatoid arthritis, so any hikes they took had to be very short. Her husband, Darwin, gave me directions for the shortcut road. He said that although it was an old logging road and so it was rough and rocky, we could make it in our Travellall. He also said he had never dared drive the Fourth of July Creek Road.

The next day the kids and I set out for Hell Roaring Lake, but the first thing that happened was we got stuck in the creek when the engine died

Darwin hadn't warned me the road forded Hell Roaring Creek near the beginning. I drove fast through the ford to be sure we wouldn't get stuck. Driving fast made a splash big enough to kill the engine. It refused to start again. I sat there a moment listening to the creek muttering along beneath the floorboards. Why didn't I drive slower? There ought to be a bridge!

Opening the car door, Doug said, "I'll go see what's the matter."

He hopped out and opened the hood.

A couple of minutes later he showed me a dripping spark plug. "The spark plugs are wet," he said, "Do you have anything to dry them with?"

"I don't think so, just Stuart s diapers, and he's going to need them."

"Maybe those campers in that trailer over there have something."

Neal opened the back door of the car, and I said, "No you stay IN the car."

Doug walked over to a trailer a hundred yards downstream where someone loaned him a roll of paper towels. After he finished drying the spark plugs, the car started right up.

Soon road dust billowed up from between cantaloupe-sized rocks, and as we crossed a hump, the car hit bottom. Since I knew the Hunts had driven the road I continued, the car bouncing and clunking. Soon the road leveled out, but the boulders grew to the size of Thanksgiving turkeys. A mostly buried one was the size of a Volkswagen Beetle and it scraped the underside of the car with a skreek. People were crazy to drive up this! Yet it was either bad roads or much longer hikes. I couldn't take longer hikes with a two year old and a four year old.

It took an hour to drive the 5 miles from the highway to the trailhead. At the end of the road next to the creek, the older children burst out of the car. I unzipped

Stuart from his seat-belt harness and set him on the ground. Then I doled out sunburn cream and mosquito repellant, tied on my sunbonnet and put on the hikeapoose. Doug stuffed our lunches, Hilary and Stuart's life jackets, and two ponchos for a rain shelter into his backpack.

Stuart's face turned bright red and he screamed and kicked when Doug tried to lower him into the hikeapoose. "No 'poose. Me walk!" he squealed.

Crossing the creek from the parking lot to the main trail required balancing on a heap of logs. Doug carried Stuart across piggyback and then went back to get his pack. Neal fell in up to his waist. On the other side when we started walking, Stuart kept stopping to look at things like beetles and horse manure. When we saw tiny red berries on low bushes and I said they were edible, the kids kept picking and eating so long I thought we'd never go on to the lake. A dead porcupine required much study and explaining. To keep the older kids amused I started telling stories about two imaginary children, David and Rachel, who lived in Sawtooth City in the mining days The remains of the city were less than ten miles from our cabin. I got the idea but not the plot from Helen Markley Miller's book, *Ski the Mountain*. Leslie had recently bought that book from a school book club.

When at last we crossed the bridge over Hell Roaring's outlet, we saw a zigzag of peaks at the head of the lake leading to a finger-like tower. It rose from a granite fist. Below these crags, columns of subalpine firs struggled up the watercourses toward bare granite slopes. Between us and the blue oval of the lake, silvery logs were scattered on marsh grass. The beauty of this scene began to fill a hole somewhere inside me. As we gazed, Stuart pointed and said, "Mounts, nice!"

How great! Even Stuart noticed. I looked at the map and pointed out the big tower. "That's the Finger of Fate," I said.

Hilary giggled, waving one hand at the tower, "Oh, the Pickle Finger of Fate. It's the one on Laugh In!"

Then she pointed to another tower. This one was black and apricot colored with a square base and triangular top. "What's that rock called, the one like a house?" she asked.

When I didn't know, she said, "It's House Rock because it looks like a house," and with a glare at Neal, added, "My House Rock." He had annoyed her on the June trip at Alturas Lake by claiming two white peaks of the White Clouds were "his" white mountains because he had seen them first. We spent the afternoon at Hell Roaring. The three older kids caught fish and Hilary and Stuart sailed stick boats from a beach of muddy sand. On the hike out it started raining, and I began to feel sick to my stomach. Back at the cabin I was so sick I had to show Doug and Leslie how to clean their fish while lying on my bed. I put the guts in a dishpan Leslie brought me. In spite of these difficulties, I thought it had been a successful hike and had been worth the effort.

The next week, when Wayne arrived, the kids insisted on hiking to Hell Roaring Lake again so he could see it. The road was just as bad but we didn't get stuck. Now the road has been shortened and the hike lengthened by a mile but the road is still just as bad even though the Forest Service once tried to upgrade it. When the kids took Wayne to Hell Roaring, they enjoyed it even more than they had the first time. It was a great hike but I was disappointed it was the only short hike we had found so far. There must be others, and I was determined to find them.

Grandpa's cabin at Fallen Leaf, CA. Margaret on the right. (photo by Wallace Cathcart)

CHAPTER 2: EDGE OF THE WORLD

One of my first memories is of a trip with my parents, Wallace and Eleanor Cathcart, to Yosemite when I was about three. My Grandma Ola, my mother's mother, and her friend Nellie from her teaching days, went with us. I sat in the back seat of our old green car with my grandma and Aunt Nellie. The gasoline smell of the car made me feel sick to my stomach. After Ola's husband, my grandfather Edwin, died she and Nellie had ridden the train for 72 hours from upstate New York to Palo Alto, where we lived in a two-bedroom house half a block from Rinconada Park. They lived in a rented house four blocks from my parents. Grandpa Edwin had lost his bank in the Depression and their house had been foreclosed on. He hadn't lived much longer after that. Grandma Ola was my favorite grandma because she played dolls with me and made up stories about what the dolls were doing. She was very thin with gray hair pinned back in a bun with big golden-brown hairpins. That day I was too carsick to play much with Grandma and my rubber doll, Dorothy. The doll was wearing grandma's handkerchief because I had thrown up on her dress. The smells made me feel like throwing up again.

As my father drove up into the hills with their scattered gray-green pine trees, we came to a lot of dump trucks and big yellow machines. A man in gray overalls and a yellow bowl-shaped hat waved a stop sign at us. When my father rolled down the window, the man said, "It'll probably be another hour."

My father asked "How far does the work continue?"

"There's another control just before the White Wolf Lodge and that will take a couple of hours. You better stay overnight there because there is NOTHING beyond it."

Nothing! The world ended just beyond the lodge and if we drove beyond it our car and all of us in it would fall off? My mother had told me the earth was round but I didn't believe her. I had seen its edge beyond the fields before we started up into the hills. The rest of the afternoon I peeked out the windows looking for the control, imagining it as a monster like a giant road machine with big eyes and long arms but I saw only bulldozers and dump trucks and after a long time another man with a stop sign. In late afternoon we came to a big brown building with little cabins around it. We stayed all night in a couple of the cabins. That night I had nightmares about falling off into a big darkness just beyond the cabins.

Next morning when we started driving beyond the White Wolf Lodge instead of turning back, I started screaming. I don't remember our driving into Yosemite Valley and seeing the waterfalls on that trip. I just remember my terror of falling off the edge of the world. Sometimes I think I am still looking for the edge to keep from falling off.

I think my father must have showed me a map of Yosemite to get me to calm down because after that trip, according to a letter from my father to my grandfather, who was on sabbatical at Duke University that year. I began to draw maps. More than 50 years later I saw the letter after my parents died. It said, "When I asked her what the little square on her map was, she replied, 'That's the little house where you ask which way to go." Probably I meant the park entrance station.

My first memory of a map is of a painted plaster relief map in the lodge at Fallen Leaf Lake near the summer cabin my grandfather had built with his own hands in 1912. I was fascinated by the relief map and loved to run my hands from its painted blue lakes up its pointed peaks when Fritzi Craven, the lodge owner, wasn't looking.

I look back on these memories to figure out why I became so obsessed with being in the mountains, not with climbing them, just with being in them. One reason is the many walks and hikes with my parents and grandfather and cabin neighbors. Most of these hikes were near my grandfather's cabin, but some were in the hills above Palo Alto. The first expedition I can remember took place when I was less than two because we still lived in a little brown house on Perry Lane out behind Stanford. (The little brown houses on Perry Lane later became famous when Jerry Garcia and other members of the Grateful Dead lived in some of them.)

That day we saw fields of California poppies in bloom. The yellow-orange flowers stretched all the way from dark trees on pale green ridges to trains chugging along like big black caterpillars. That day my grandmother Edna, still had short, dark hair and big buttons down the front of her long dress. My grandfather Arthur wore a woolly jacket and he still had hair and it was pale orange. I also remember my Uncle Bob that day with his whirring movie camera. My grandfather pulled me out into the poppies in my red wagon. I was amazed at so much orange. I remember thinking the poppies smelled like old milk. The only wild poppies today are in parks in the coastal hills west of Palo Alto and there are only scattered patches.

From the time I was small my parents took me, my brother Tom, and sister Dodie on walks and hikes near home but the best hikes were from my grandfather's cabin at Fallen Leaf Lake near Lake Tahoe. On the maps of California, Fallen Leaf is the blue drop below the south end of Tahoe that makes it look as though Tahoe has sprung a leak. We always spent my father's two-week vacations at that cabin. Even the route my father took to Fallen Leaf was special. It followed back roads. At the south end of Tahoe, we passed the lodge and cabins of Camp Richardson. Just beyond it, we turned onto a paved one-lane road to Fallen Leaf Lake and around it. On the way we passed a view of the mountain called Tallac, which had a cross of snow on it. For years its photo appeared at the beginning of the TV program Bonanza. Recently I learned that the lake may have been named for a Delaware chief who guided Colonel Cock-eye Johnson as he explored the Sierras in the 1850s. Or it may have been named for an old folk song about an Indian maiden named Falling Leaf. The road passed below cabins and above boat docks.

Soon we looked into the U-shaped entrance and high peaks of Glen Alpine Canyon. Even in summer a cold wind often blew down it and out over the lake, raising whitecaps. Next to the canyon huddled a clutch of brown board cabins that my parents called The Housekeeping Camp because each cabin had a cookstove and sink. The camp also had a store and cafe. Between the cabins and the lake grew immense sugar pines with foot-long cones that were covered with pitch.

The last bit of the drive was up the Stanford Hill on a road paved only in the wheel tracks and not in the middle. The eleven cabins near the top were the ones built by my grandfather and ten professor friends around 1912. They took out the first permit for summer cabins on the Eldorado National Forest in 1910. It cost them $250 a year for the whole 17 acres at first, about $23 apiece. Grandpa was one of the original professors in the Stanford Law School when David Starr Jordan started it in 1904. Jordan had come to Colorado Springs where my grandfather was reading law to recruit him because Grandpa had been such a good debater as a Stanford student. Grandpa's parents had moved from Iowa to Colorado Springs to take part in the Cripple Creek mining boom. Grandpa met my grandma, Edna, when she came to visit her parents who had moved there for her mother's health.

After my grandfather finished the 10 by 10 foot kitchen, the only room he built in 1912, my grandmother and their three little boys came up on the train to Truckee, rode a narrow gauge railroad to Tahoe City, then the steamer Tahoe to Tallac Lodge, and from there rode a horse-drawn wagon to the cabin. Afterwards Grandma Edna wrote in her diary: "Had fine trip on train to Tahoe where Arthur is building us a shack." It was no wonder she didn't sound more excited. The boys were then only one, three, and five. My father, who was five, remembered pounding in some nails and pinching his toe in the loose boards of the tent floor. My grandfather hadn't yet built a platform for the big tent.

My parents seemed happier at Fallen Leaf than at home and spent more time with us kids there. My brother Tom was three years younger than I and my sister Dodie is six years younger. We did the household tasks like getting wood for the stove together, and they played board games and visited the neighbors with us. They also took us to the beach or on a hike every day. I think my mother was both bored and frazzled as a housewife. None of the modern conveniences like automatic washers, dryers, dishwashers, and frozen foods had yet been invented. My mother had worked for the Federal Reserve Board in Washington DC for three years before she got married. There she had edited the employee newsletter. Going to Fallen Leaf must have been a good change of scene from housework for her, especially since she had grown up going to her grandfather's cottage on Lake Bomoseen in southern Vermont every summer. I think my father much preferred hiking, taking pictures and counting wildflowers, to figuring how much income tax his firm's clients owed. He had started out as an economics instructor at Stanford but had been laid off because of the Depression. The rest of his life he worked as a C.P.A. in San Francisco, commuting on the train. Beginning in 1955 my mother worked as an accountant for *Sunset*.

When I was a child the cabin was two small brown buildings with green shingle roofs and orange shutters. One was a kitchen, living room, and bedroom and the other was a two-bedroom bunkhouse. At the back of a large deck, faucets watched over a gray unpainted bench with washbasins on it. Next to it water dripped onto a burlap sack on top of a mortared stone cooler that served as the cabin refrigerator. Above the cooler a dozen stone steps and a path led to an outhouse. It had a flush toilet that drained into a cesspool next to the path. From the cabin we could see a blue wedge of lake, and a wooded ridge behind it. We also looked across Glen Alpine Canyon at Indian Rock which had granite eyebrows and nose and a warbonnet of trees.

As a small child at Fallen Leaf what I liked to do best was pad down the hill road in my sneakers a quarter mile to Baby Beach. It was called that because the smaller children used it while the older ones swam at the beach and dock at the Housekeeping Camp. Above Baby Beach rose a steep sandy bank, topped by the red branches and round leaves of manzanita bushes. My father showed me that if I picked a leaf and pinched it, it smelled like apple pie. One reason I loved to go to the beach is that afterwards we always walked along the lake road to Fallen Leaf Lodge for double cones of Chism ice cream. It was an especially rich ice cream made in Reno. Over both beaches wafted a sweet smell. When I grew up I learned it was made of manzanita, snowbrush, Jeffrey pine, and incense cedar. This combination of smells could still lead me to Fallen Leaf blindfolded, the way a spawning salmon smells out the stream where it hatched.

I also liked to go with my father to visit the neighbors. On one side of Grandpa's cabin there was the cabin of Grosvenor, a childhood friend of my father, who was a professor of harmony in Chicago, and his wife Adit (spelled Edith) who played the violin. On the other side of Grandpa's cabin was the Elmore s cottage with its octagonal living room. The mother, Mary Jane, and her son John would stay all summer, and I liked to go there to watch her clock change numbers. It was the first clock like it that I had seen. John had something the matter with him, possibly autism, and had to be coaxed to do anything. Down the Hill there was Bobbie Fish who sat on her porch in a sun hat that was three-feet wide and told us all the news about everyone on the hill. If we didn't stop and talk to her she would get up and follow us until we did. But most of all I liked to go with my father and Tom to visit Mills Waterhouse, the local handyman and hermit. One side of his cabin was covered with mousetraps with bits of paper in them. He told us it was his filing system. The papers recorded how much each client owed him. We loved to hear the tales of his adventures, like how he had to drive his Model T up Tioga Pass near Yosemite in reverse so enough gas would get into the engine to make it to the top of the pass.

By the time I was seven or eight I felt more excited the night before we went to Fallen Leaf than I was the night before Christmas. I couldn't even sleep. Once at the cabin I worried about wild animals, but I began to believe the world was actually round.

When my parents began to take me on hikes that weren't just walks I didn't like them at first. I thought they were too hard and too long - my legs ached, my eyes hurt from the sun, and it was way too hot. The first of these long hikes was a climb of Tallac, the mountain above Fallen Leaf with the snow cross. I remember complaining about the trail being too hard when we had gone only a few hundred yards above the trailhead at Glen Alpine. My father had made me taste the nasty, sulphur tasting water of the spring, and I was already annoyed with him for that. As we started up the trail the dust from his feet made me choke. I asked, "When are we going to get there?"

"It'll be awhile, but you can have some lifesavers and water when we cross the creek in about five minutes," my father said, holding out a shiny white rock toward me. "Here's something you might like. It's a piece of quartz."

The little rock sparkled. Quartz, I thought, like a quart of milk. It even looked like milk.

All the rest of the hike I picked up every sparkling rock -- white, pink, and orange -- and stuffed them in the pockets of my pink cotton pants. Although the rocks wore holes in my pockets and sandpapered my thighs, trying to find pretty rocks propelled me all the way up the mountain. Eventually we saw nothing higher ahead except for hundreds of butterflies. They were orange with black spots and they fluttered in the air and on the rocks with a faint whisper. They were so pretty it seemed as though I was imagining them.

When I looked down I saw Fallen Leaf Lake. It didn't look like the leaf on the lodge letter paper as I expected. Instead it resembled a blue-green boot print stamped into a fluffy dark green rug next to the immense pale blue plate of Lake Tahoe.

While we ate lunch, a chipmunk stole my parents friend's sandwich. Absorbed in their conversation, no one except me noticed the chipmunk until he and the sandwich were several yards away and I had started laughing.

"You should have said something!" said my mother, with a twist of her mouth. My mother scolded me and made me give the lady the cookies from my lunch.

In bed that night, trails and pine trees moved along behind my eyelids and kept me awake, but I felt proud of myself. I had climbed a mountain, so I was a big girl, but it was too much hard work. A couple of days later when my parents asked me to go up another mountain I said no thank you. I had already climbed one and that was enough.

I thought my dad's vacation was too short. We always spent it at my grandfather's cabin. I hated to go home at the end of the vacation. I don't know how old I was, maybe five or six when I remember coming down the stone steps from the toilet onto the gray board deck to hear my mother calling, "Margy, we're leaving. Get in the car, now." Instead of walking across the deck to the front steps, I sneaked in the back door of the main cabin. As I tiptoed I drew in the smell of the incense cedar tree whose feathery branches hung over the door. Its smell was mixed with the faint urine smell of the white enamel chamber pots that had been rinsed and put under the tree to air. In the back bedroom I glided between the twin beds covered with khaki blankets that said U.S. on them. I didn't want to go home. At home I couldn't even cross the street to play with other kids. I wanted Fallen Leaf to go on longer. When I reached the hallway between the living room and kitchen I heard my mother calling again, so I hid beside the silver paper covered water heater in its little closet. My father soon found me and dragged me out. I had thought they wouldn't find me and I could just stay there.

When I was seven, my parents talked me into going on a hike from Echo Lake to Fallen Leaf. The hike would start with a motorboat ride, and many of the neighbors were going. My father said there were lots of rocks to collect, and we were not going to climb a mountain, so it sounded like fun. I loved the boat ride, but I was so slow that the rest of the group soon got way ahead of us. They were finishing lunch by the time we reached them at Lake Aloha in Desolation Valley. By then it had clouded over. I wondered why we had come so far to see a big gray lake enclosed by pale rocks studded by big white sticks. I would later learn that the sticks were dead trees killed by the rise in water level from a small stone dam built in the 1920s. Soon after we arrived, the neighbors finished their lunches and got up and left. After we ate lunch and started on again, my mother walked ahead and put lifesavers on rocks so I would hike faster.

On the way to Fallen Leaf from there, a huge thunderstorm came up. The thunder hurt my ears and lightning struck a little ridge right above us. It was so close it made a funny smell and turned the white rock along the trail pink. I remember how cold I was, but how much fun it was to splash my shoes in the puddles. I wasn't afraid of the lightning and thunder because my parents didn't act afraid. They must have been though, because when I told my mother I had to go to the bathroom, she said, "We can't stop. Just wet your pants. It won't matter because you're already so wet."

When we got to the usual trailhead at Glen Alpine, we still had two more miles to go down the road and a cutoff path to reach the cabin. We stopped and rested for a few minutes, but we were so cold my mother made me and my dad do jumping jacks with her to ward off what she called exposure. Doing jumping jacks with sore muscles really hurt, but it made me feel a little warmer.

I had not enjoyed that hike, but each year there were more hikes to go on, most of them with cabin neighbors and their children. My father was like a pied piper of hikers. He would go to every cabin of the ten other professors and invite people to go on hikes. So there were always other kids and interesting adults on the hikes.

In contrast at home in Palo Alto and at school I didn't get along as well or feel as happy as I did at Fallen Leaf. For example, when the Japanese bombed Pearl Harbor and World War II started my parents shooed me outside away from the radio. When I went to school the next day and the teacher talked about the war that had started, I raised my hand and said there wasn't either a war. The kids laughed at me and kept teasing me about being a baby. I was only in the first grade, so that didn't get me off to a good start in school. I didn't catch on to how to read right away either and that added to my feeling of being different. When I asked my mother why they hadn't told me about the war, she said they hadn't wanted to frighten me.

Pastel cotton dresses with puffed sleeves were the fashion for little girls then, but my Grandma Cathcart made my dresses of dark, practical colors and none had puffed sleeves. Other girls made comments about my clothes and that made me feel even more set apart. The girls in my class all lived across a busy street called Embarcadero, so the couple of times I was invited to go play with one of them after school my parents wouldn't let me go, and for this reason, I was never allowed to invite any of them. So they formed their own friendships that didn't include me.

These things made the two weeks at Fallen Leaf sparkle compared to the rest of the year at home. My parents continued to take us up mountains that had trails to the top or were easy scrambles. My dad had us count how many mountains we had climbed, and that inspired me to climb more. He carved our initials in a big log near the cabin and had us carve a dot beside them for each mountain. We also hiked to various lakes.

The summer I was ten my father took me on my first overnight hike. I felt special to be the only child in the family who was invited. My sleeping bag was pocked with bullet-sized holes when my father brought it home from an army surplus store, but my mother had patched the holes. The bag cost little because of the holes, but I worried that a soldier had been shot in it. My father's bag had no holes.

As we prepared for the overnight, my father showed me how to roll and tie the cloth ties around the sleeping bag by keeping one knee on the rolled part. Then I stuffed the bag, my sweater, and a roll of toilet paper into my little gray-green knapsack. He stowed the food, cooking pot, ground cloths and his sleeping bag into a triangular army-surplus pack. With it on, he looked like a turtle with a deformed shell.

Usually, lots of people wanted to go on my father's hikes, but this time he had to search below the ten cabins to find anyone. From the cabin at the lowest hairpin turn in the road, he recruited two hikers. One was sixteen-year-old Alison, whose red hair matched the frames of her glasses. The other was Mrs. Bird, her family's gray-haired, leathery houseguest.

We began the hike north of Fallen Leaf at Meeks Bay on Lake Tahoe. When we started out, the straps of my knapsack chewed on my collar bones even with the makeshift pads my father had rigged out of sanitary napkins and bandannas. I was embarrassed by the pads, but didn't complain because I was so excited about going on an overnight hike.

By the time we neared the summit of the trail at Phipps Pass, my legs and head ached. After two more hours we reached Middle Velma Lake, 11 miles from the car. By then I was so sore it felt as though my legs extended up to my ribs.

At sunset, salmon-pink light lit up the tops of different peaks in succession, as though a fire burned briefly inside each one. Shading his eyes from the glare, my father said this light was called the alpenglow. Dust near the earth's surface caused it by scattering all colors of the sunlight except red. The alpenglow appeared only when there was something high for the setting sun to shine upon. It seemed like magic to me and still does.

When the pink dimmed to gray-blue, my father built a fire and we moved from rocks to logs around it to avoid the smoke. My father loved to sing and he led us in rousing songs like *A Capital Ship for An Ocean Trip Was the Walloping Window Blind*. In between the songs, I listened to the stream whispering between the two lakes.

Before bedtime, we scampered up a dome-shaped white outcrop, the rubber soles of our sneakers sticking to the rock enough to let us walk straight up it. From the top we watched the reflection of the full moon on the lake. As the wind ruffled the water, and the moon pearl changed to a rippling white path, I felt a deep peace.

On the way back to Fallen Leaf the next day we scrambled cross-country up a stream that slid over smooth granite in thin sheets. My father called it a water slide. Above it was a lake called Fontanalis. Around its turquoise water, white outcrops, and red and white mountain heather formed a dramatic border. Today the Pacific Crest Trail goes right by Fontanalis, but there was no trail to it then.

That trip showed me so many beautiful things mountains held that I fell in love with mountains. Hiking began to seem the best activity in the world.

The only trouble was that the months between my dad's summer vacations were much too long. After Thanksgiving dinner at my grandparents house that fall, I was sitting on the couch while my grandfather, father and uncles discussed law. I figured it was at least seven more months until we went to Fallen Leaf again and sighed. Grandpa noticed me sitting there and came over and sat down beside me. He asked how school was going. "OK I guess, but it's too long until next summer when we can go to Fallen Leaf again." I pulled at my wool plaid skirt, which was itching my legs.

My grandfather limped over to a built-in bookcase, drew out two leather-covered books and said, "Here is something that might keep you going until next summer. John Muir writes about the Sierra so well you ll feel the mountains are in your living room."

I loved to read, but I didn't see how some old books could shorten the time until the next summer. At school everything had begun to change. I used to enjoy answering the teachers' questions but my classmates had begun to laugh at me when I answered questions.

How could dusty old books take away my hollow feeling? My grandfather handed me Volume I of Muir's *The Mountains of California*. With my index finger I traced the gold letters on its spine. The book smelled forbidden, like the locked trunks my mother kept in the garage.

"Thank you, Grandpa," I said. I knew John Muir had a trail named after him, but little else. Then I remembered my father saying Muir was a fraud because he said he only took bread and tea on his hiking trips. My dad had said that in between trips he went to visit ranchers in the Owens Valley and stuffed himself with their food for free.

My grandfather said that Muir helped make Yosemite a national park. He wrote books about the Sierras and he founded the Sierra Club.

I opened the book and began to examine the pictures and read a line here and there. I was thrilled to find beautiful descriptions of mountains.

Muir's big words painted pictures of waterfalls and wildflowers. They let me feel as though I breathed mist, smelled flowers and ran my hands over smooth, warm granite. I loved Muir's images and sounds, such as this sentence I found, "Seeing the sunbursts of morning among the icy peaks, the noonday radiance on the trees and rocks and snow, the flush of the alpenglow, and a thousand dashing waterfalls with their marvelous abundance of irised spray, it still seems to me above all others the Range of Light." When I found out more about Muir, and how he spent so many summers in the mountains, I wished I could be like him. I wanted to live in the mountains and write about them like he did. When I told my mother what I wanted to do, she said writers didn't make any money and I should instead do something more useful when I grew up. When I told my father about what I wanted to do, he suggested that since I liked to collect rocks I could be a geologist. He told me that geologists often worked in the mountains.

Margaret with Margaret and Carrie Brown.
(photo by Wallace Cathcart)

CHAPTER 3: MT SILL

When I was in the eighth grade I met Margaret Brown. Her family had a little cabin at Lily Lake only a mile from Fallen Leaf and spent the whole summer there. The summer after I met her, we began to go on hikes with her and her family. By then my mother took Tom, Dodie, and me up to Fallen Leaf as soon as school ended in June before my father's vacation in July. Margaret was a year behind me in school and had attended a different elementary school, so I hadn't known her before. She was very enthusiastic and often said, "That's wonderful!," her green eyes glowing. At school I was impressed with the poems she wrote, which sounded like the ones in our English book. She said she wanted to be a writer. Having Margaret at Fallen Leaf to go hiking and to the beach with made all the difference to me during my teenage summers. I probably would have felt bored if she hadn't been there. My parents let me invite two or three other friends to Fallen Leaf for a week each year, but I would have been lonely the rest of the vacations without other kids my age. There were other teens at Fallen Leaf, but their cabins were along the lake road and their families had motor boats. They also were not from Palo Alto, so I didn't know them.

The first hike with Margaret and her family was to a big snowbank about a mile above Lily Lake right under the face of the Indian Rock. Algae tinted the snow pink here and there. We threw snowballs and then built a snowman, which Carrie, Margaret's little sister, insisted be a snow lady with bosoms. Margaret contributed her yellow sunbonnet for a hat. Tom found an old ladder in the rocks that had been made into a sled. It had strips of steel nailed along the edges on one side for runners. We pushed and dragged the sled to the top of the snowbank and took turns riding it down. First Tom sat on the sled and we pushed him off, swoosh. He kept his feet out to the sides to use as brakes, but let the sled careen down to the hollow at the base of the snowbank. By the time we had to hike back to our cabin,, the ladder sled was falling apart. So that winter Tom built a sled and painted it green. He called it The Green Mariah. The next summer we carried it up to the snowbank. We kept it hidden in the forest below the snowbank, and used it every summer for several years. We took many other hikes with the Browns, including overnights where we climbed some of the peaks of the Crystal Range in Desolation Valley, including Agazzi and Aloha.

In the spring of my junior year in high school, I was delighted when my father said he planned a family pack trip. Polishing his glasses, he said, "I've asked Margaret's father if they'd like to go on a pack trip with us this summer and he said yes."

"That's wonderful!" I said. "Where are we going to go?"

"I thought we'd go into the Evolution Country, I think that is the most beautiful place on the Muir Trail."

My father pulled the map out of his Starr's *Guide to the Muir Trail* and showed me the route we would take above Bishop, California. It led from North Lake over Piute Pass to the Muir Trail, along it and then over Bishop Pass to South Lake.

I had heard for years about my father's two Muir Trail burro trips, and the previous spring he had started planning a burro trip for us. We hadn't taken it, though, because while building a fence around the backyard he tripped over a pile of lumber one evening and broke his ankle.

To prepare for our trip, we drove 60 miles from Fallen Leaf to Carson City to buy a paraffin-covered wheel of cheddar cheese and an unsliced side of bacon still in its rind. We needed enough food for five people for 14 days and my father had me help him plan the quantities. The Browns were bringing their own food.

To begin the trip, the families drove south along U.S. 395 in two cars. It was July 11 and hot. Our car boiled several times on the steep winding road that led through the sagebrush from Bishop to the packer's place at Lake Sabrina. Each time it boiled we waited until it cooled off enough to open the radiator. Then my father added more water from the wool plaid-covered automobile canteen. When the water ran out he climbed down to the creek to fill the canteen. At Lake Sabrina, we arranged to rent four burros: two white ones, Mama and Angel, a black burro named Baby, and a brown one named Maneater. The family who had raised Maneater had named him that for his love of nuzzling people to search for treats. As I rubbed the burros noses, it was hard for me to believe that these awkward-looking animals were strong enough to carry all our stuff for two weeks. The packer, Art Schober, considered Maneater the most difficult burro. My father assigned one burro to each child. That meant Dodie and Carrie had to share one. I thought it would be easy to lead Maneater, but the first day, on the way from the trailhead at North Lake to Piute Lake, he walked so fast I fell and skinned my shins. He also tried to knock off his load against trees.

Descending the far side of Piute Pass on the second day, the burro Angel rolled off the trail. I had walked ahead with Maneater, followed by Tom with Baby, and Margaret with Mama, so I didn't see Angel fall. We only heard the screams from Dodie and Carrie, who were leading Angel. I gave Maneater to Tom and hurried back up the trail to see what had happened, for we thought someone was hurt. Luckily, Angel only had a little cut on her leg and the stuff she was carrying wasn't damaged. It took Leland Brown several minutes to get Angel back up on the trail and put ointment and a bandage on her leg.

After that we spent three days in the rain, first at a lake called Golden Trout. It was at timberline and surrounded by white granite peninsulas studded with a few whitebark pines. Above it on the north across a vast basin of white granite and small lakes rose the cliffs of Mt. Humphrey. In the rain my father took a picture of six of us sitting under the pitched life raft sail that we used as a tent. A friend of my dad later used that photo in a book on Yosemite. In between showers we caught so many golden trout and another party gave us so many we had fish for every meal.

On the sixth day, we had to ford Evolution Creek to continue to Muir Pass and complete our loop trip. I had trouble keeping my footing as I waded through the waist-deep creek. The fathers led the little girls across and then the three smaller burros. Baby, the smallest burro, started to float downstream at one point but caught herself and stumbled on across. Wet food and sleeping bags would be a calamity here in this country, which was much colder than what we were used to near Fallen Leaf. As I put my jeans, sox, and high basketball shoes back on at the far side of the ford I watched my father trying to get Maneater to walk into the creek. If the burros couldn't cross the ford, we couldn't complete our loop trip, so I was worried. My father waded into the creek in his boxer shorts, drew Maneater's rope around his waist for leverage and pulled. As Leland, in rolled-up jeans, swatted the burro from behind, with an "Ay-Ya", Maneater stepped sideways, then forward into the creek where he stopped and wouldn't budge.

I was afraid the current would sweep Maneater away. Then my father led Maneater back up onto the bank. On our side of the creek Leland untied the ropes from the three burros and then tied them together into one long rope. He threw one end of it across the creek to my father, who tied it to Maneater's halter.

Leland, wrapped one end of the joined ropes around a big lodgepole pine at the edge of the creek and began to pull. Back on the other side of the creek, my father swatted Maneater on the rump.

Little by little Maneater stumbled out into the creek. In just a few steps the water reached halfway up the sides of his wooden pack boxes. Leland hauled on the rope so hard he leaned over each time Maneater stumbled forward and the loosened rope snaked towards him. The water against the boxes began to drop, and at last Maneater clattered out of the water. I remember stroking Maneater's nose and saying, "You're the best burro in the whole world. That was really deep and you did it."

On the eighth day, we camped at Evolution Lake to prepare for the 14-mile stretch over the highest point on the trail, 12,059-foot Muir Pass. We planned to hike 14 miles between camps because the trail ran above timberline where there was no firewood. Camping was not allowed in those 14 miles except in an emergency.

At Evolution Lake we camped between white granite benches at the edge of a meadow. This lake huddled beneath the massive pleats and furrows of mountains called Darwin and Huxley. I thought I never before had seen such a beautiful place. At sunset after drying the dinner dishes, Margaret and I scrambled up a granite knoll to watch the alpenglow. We wanted to get away from the others so we could talk about boys without Tom, Dodie, Carrie or the parents listening. In the granite crevices of the knoll, magenta Muir primroses still bloomed. It was silent except for the distant thwack of an axe and the soft clang of burro bells from our camp.

The next day we arose before dawn, and started out for Muir Pass at 8 A.M., three hours before we usually left. That day we led the burros over treeless granite and through basins laden with blue lakes. Each of us carried a stick of wood in one hand and left it in the stone emergency shelter on top of Muir Pass, for those who might need the sticks for lifesaving warmth.

On the other side of the pass, the trail dropped to timberline in the wooded chasm of LeConte Canyon. We camped in the canyon for two nights and then climbed out of it to the Dusty Lakes.

Just before supper that evening a grubby old man walked into our camp. My father was off taking pictures, Leland and Tom were fishing Dodie and Carrie were down at the lake catching frogs, and my mother was getting water. Louise Brown was cooking over the campfire. The man had gray hair down to his shoulders and a long beard. He wore patched pants and a dirty white long underwear shirt but his boots looked new and freshly polished. He introduced himself as Norman Clyde and said he was helping with a wilderness camp for boys that was run by his friend Jules Eichorn.

"That sure smells good. All Jules ever fixes is beans and boiled macaroni."

The man seemed so strange I wished he'd go away but he stood there talking about the camp and their adventures. His eyes focused on Louise s hand as she stirred our lima beans and ham. After a few minutes she noticed him watching and gave him a plate of our beans.

After he had taken a bite he said it was delicious. Before he had finished the beans, another man, a bit younger, came up and told Mr. Clyde he needed help with the camp's dinner. That man was Jules Eichorn and he resembled a collection of steel wires topped by a lined and tanned face and sun-streaked hair. He invited us to come to their campfire that evening.

When we went to their camp Eichorn took my Dad's topographic nap and showed us the route up Mt. Sill, the 14,159-foot mountain that we planned to climb the next day. "You better not try to take those little girls up the mountain," he said, one wiry arm pointing to Dodie and Carrie. "It's too hard for them and you can't take the burros into Palisades Basin. There's no grass."

After we started back to our camp , my father said, "Those two are the most famous climbers in the Sierras. They made many of the first ascents including the east face of Mt. Whitney which is all cliffs."

Wow, meeting these men was like meeting John Muir himself.

Clyde reminded me of Mills Waterhouse, the bald and overalled handyman who lived at Fallen Leaf all summer and fall. Mills seemed exciting because he stayed at Fallen Leaf so much of the year and because my mother wouldn't let us go visit him without my father. By the time of the Muir Trail trip I knew people considered Mills strange, maybe even crazy. Clyde reminded me of how much I wanted to live in the mountains but I didn't want to be grubby and strange the way he and Mills were. According to kids from first grade on being strange was a horrible fate. There wasn't the appreciation then for people, especially women, who do unusual things.

The next afternoon my father, Leland, Margaret, Tom and I started off for Knapsack Pass, a saddle above the head of the Dusy Lake basin. As we worked our way past the string of small lakes on the way to the pass, the added weight of our sleeping bags, food, and extra clothes in our knapsacks felt like paving stones on our backs. The knapsacks didn't have any waistbands to shift part of the weight onto our hips as packs today have.

On the other side of the pass in Palisades Basin, we were enclosed by mountains with cliffs. We camped on hard sand between rocks, so I didn't sleep much. Mostly I lay awake examining the stars, listening to the trilling stream, thinking about the early climbers like Whymper and Muir and Clyde and worrying whether we'd reach the top of Mt. Sill.

Before dawn we breakfasted by firelight, taking turns with Leland's squeeze-powered flashlight so he could stir the oatmeal and spoon it into our aluminum cups. Leland taught illumination engineering and a colleague had invented the flashlight. Leaving our camping gear wrapped in a life raft sail, we climbed over a pass. Then we followed the canyon of Glacier Creek to two unnamed lakes in the rocks.

At the lakes, my father handed me the topographic map and asked me to lead, saying I needed to learn to find the way using a topographic map. I was happy to oblige, pleased my father thought me experienced enough to take the lead. On the map, the contour lines looked farther apart to the far left where I could see ledges than they did over the huge boulders straight ahead. However, the ledges turned out to be cliffs. "This is the wrong way," Tom complained, grabbing the map from me, "Mr. Eichorn didn't say there were any cliffs."

When I failed to find an easy way up the first cliff, and we sat down to rest, Leland began rummaging in his knapsack, "If it's this hard, Margaret and I are going to turn back. Here, I'm going to give you some of our food. You ll need it."

Breaking off a bit of chocolate, Margaret said, "I don't want to go back, Papa."

My father waved away the food and said, "We're going to turn around and go back and try a different route."

It upset me and I stared at the map trying to see where I had gone the wrong way. The trek out to the cliffs used up two hours. Had my stupidity meant we wouldn't get to the top? My father insisted I keep leading, but I didn't want to be responsible for the climb's failure. Only after I led us back to where we started cutting over did he escort us through the boulders to the top of the saddle ahead. The boulders proved much easier than my route -- topographic maps evidently were deceptive.

My father got out the directions for Mt. Sill that he had copied from Starr's *Guide to the Muir Trail* and read them to us. "From the head of Glacier Creek you boldly and blindly take the steep rocky wall on the right (east) side of the amphitheater," so my father did. At least this set of cliffs wasn't as steep as the ones I had led us to. From the top of them, however, we saw that the summit was way over to the left, not just ahead as we had thought. Somehow it had moved since I last looked at it. My father had led us too far to the right. We descended, circled, and climbed difficult pitches to reach it. My father leading us up cliffs and down made me feel better about my earlier detour.

Finally, we reached the top, Leland and Margaret, too. I felt on top of the clouds as well as the mountain. This 14,100-foot mountain, my highest ever, made me feel as though I had taken a difficult test and although I had to answer one question twice, had passed it.

A golf club stuck out of the summit cairn. Tom pulled it out and hit pebbles off the edge. This mountain was the first he had climbed for five years. I thought back to the last one, Pyramid, remembering my thirst and feeling of accomplishment. On that hike, my father had let us drink only three sips of water at each of the few streams. He said we would get stomach aches if we drank more. When he was a boy, he had gotten a very bad stomach ache on a hike and thought drinking cold water had caused it. Even so, he still refused to carry a canteen because of the weight.

Near the top of Pyramid, Tom had flopped down, his face bright red, pulled off his baseball cap and said, "I'm not going any farther without water."

I had thought him a baby, for a boy whose well-developed biceps the neighbor boys brought their friends to see. My mouth felt sandy, but a little thing like thirst wouldn't keep me from the top of the mountain. After Tom ate a few orange sections and some chocolate, he accompanied us to the summit.

On the way down Pyramid Tom scampered ahead out of sight. When my father found him face down drinking water out of a snow pond that jiggled with mosquito larvae, he scolded him for drinking bad water. Afterward, Tom had refused to climb any more mountains until this one.

As I sat on the summit of Mt. Sill, cirrus clouds spread angel hair over the sky. To the west, blue haze cloaked the Central Valley. Leland sat at the summit resting, my father wandered around taking pictures, and Margaret lay down on a flat rock and pulled her yellow sunbonnet over her face. I didn't see why she wanted to go to sleep when we had finally reached the top of this amazing mountain and could see for hundreds of miles.

I dropped to my hands and knees and crept forward to look down the sheer east face of the mountain. Dark gray crevasses split dirty gray ice on the Palisades Glacier below. I was disappointed because I thought glaciers were white with turquoise crevasses. Around me breathed the wind, and hundreds of feet below, a stream whispered. For a few minutes climbing this mountain gave me the feeling I could do anything.

When I returned to the summit, my father borrowed the golf club from Tom and used it to point out Mt. Whitney, a tiny triangle on the ridge far to the south. He described climbing it with his father and brothers 28 years earlier, before either the Muir Trail or a trail to the top existed.

After only a few minutes, my father and Leland hurried us off the summit. Even so, by the time we found our campsite it was 10:30 P.M., 14 hours after we had left it. We had passed it in the dark and had to climb back up the creek to find it. Everyone was too tired to cook, so we just ate leftover lunch and drank cocoa for supper.

In mid-morning the next day when we returned to Dusy Lakes, I was disappointed to find that my mother and Louise had everything packed up to leave. Rubbing her back, my mother said she wanted to go on out to the trailhead that day, and we did.

It was 12 miles from there out to South Lake and because I was so tired I don't remember anything about the trail.

Afterwards, I thought back to the two weeks on the Muir Trail ending in Mt. Sill as a turning point in my life. I thought the climb had given me confidence I could accomplish really difficult things.

Back in Palo Alto our school literary club published a magazine with a story I had written. It was about a little girl whose foot is trapped in rocks in the mountains. It didn't tell whether she was ever rescued. In the story I think I unconsciously showed my dilemma over whether to try to act like an ordinary young girl or to go off and spend my life in the mountains the way I dreamed of doing or to try to do both.

Margaret climbing with ropes and pitons. (photo by Tom Cathcart)

CHAPTER 4: BARRIERS

As I grew up I found that girls and women were not allowed to do certain things especially those in the outdoors and were required to do others. For example girls had to wear dresses or skirts to school even in winter. That was a minor barrier but some things were more restrictive. The first time I remember being really upset by girls not being allowed I was ten or eleven.

The community center six blocks from my house in Palo Alto included a Junior Museum where I took classes in drawing, clay modeling and rock collecting. The museum was a stucco building without the red tile roofs and little towers of the rest of the center. I wanted to take the boat building class because Tom had taken it and built a beautiful little boat that really sailed. When I tried to sign up for boat building, I was told it was only for boys. Josephine, the white-haired lady who ran the museum, asked the boat-building teacher if he'd let me join the class.

He wouldn't, so I built my own boat in my parent's garage. I used a four-by-four, a piece of galvanized steel sheeting from the site of a new house, a large fishing weight, a dowel, old sheets and string. I sawed out a boat shape from the 4-by-4, then smoothed it with a wood file and sandpaper. My father came out to the garage to see what I was doing, and said, "You can only use the workbench and my tools if you sweep up all the sawdust."

I sawed a slit in the hull and glued the sheet metal keel into it and pinched the big fishing weight onto the keel with pliers. I drilled a hole for the mast and glued the dowel into it. Then I swept up the sawdust. I painted the hull a nice bright red and sewed sails and tied them to the mast with string. When finished the boat was beautiful. My father drove me to the docks on the nearby bay so I could try it out, but it tipped over as soon as I put it in the water. It wouldn't stay upright even in the bathtub.

When I took my boat to Josephine and complained that it wouldn't stay upright, she had the boat-building teacher come and look at it. He smelled like the strange glue he cooked for the boats on a hot plate. He said, "Didn't you know that your brother's boat was made in sections that were hollowed out with a jigsaw and then glued together? Your boat is top heavy."

Josephine looked at the boat teacher with a frown and said, "I think you need to let this girl use your jigsaw and clamps to make a boat. She has worked so hard. Will you do that?"

"Yes, I guess so. I could stay after the boys leave."

Turning to me, he set his lips in a stern line. and said, "Do you want to do that?"

"No, I don't think so." I already made a boat. I thought he should have given me directions when he wouldn't let me take the class. I was still way too angry to want to work with him.

My rock collection helped me survive elementary and junior high school when my teachers and parents tried to teach me to be a lady. Ladies didn't do cartwheels because that showed their underpants. Ladies didn't try to beat up mean girls or boys who teased them. Ladies sat with their knees together. I wished I could live at Fallen Leaf where it would always be summer and I didn't have to try to be a lady.

I had collected rocks ever since the hike up Tallac when I was six. My Grandma Ola had told me there were rocks as pretty as clear Jello, so I kept looking for pretty rocks. I began entering my rock collection in the annual science fair that was sponsored by the junior museum. At first I just got a lavender ribbon for honorable mention, partly because my rocks were all different sizes. The next year I broke the big ones in pieces with a hammer, so the ones in the collection would be the same size. Then I gathered See's candy boxes, lined them with cotton from vitamin bottles, made cardboard dividers, and numbered each rock with a tiny square of adhesive tape. I then made a list of the names of the rocks and pasted it inside the cover of each box. When I added the place each rock had been found I began to get blue ribbons. When I learned that people could get jobs working with rocks and collections of them and that those who did mostly worked outdoors, often in the mountains, I decided I wanted to do this, to be a geologist when I grew up.

My father encouraged me by buying me *The Rock Book* and by bringing me rocks from some of his clients. For example one client gave him a piece of mahogany obsidian. It was black streaked with brown, and came from the Mahogany Mountains in Oregon. He also drove me to a nearby rock formation he called The Basaltic Columns. This was a huge cliff of six-sided basalt columns. I was fascinated that the lava had formed these columns as it cooled. When we were at Fallen Leaf the whole family visited the Nevada state museum in Carson City. There I was amazed by the colorful crystals and beauty of the minerals shown under what my father called black light.

Yet I never met any women who were geologists. In those days most women were stay at home mothers anyway. I wondered if a girl could be a geologist if she got married. I didn't want to be a geologist if I had to be a sad old maid like Grandma Ola's friend Nellie. Aunt Nellie was a small thin woman with wavy white hair and rimless glasses. Grandma had brought Nellie with her to California when she came West after my grandfather lost his bank in the Depression and then died. Aunt Nellie had taught high school Latin and had never married.

The only woman scientist I saw until I was grown was single, chubby, had thick glasses and very short, straight hair. I didn't want to look like her if that was what being a scientist did to you.

One evening at dinner when I was about 15, my father glanced across our polished maple dining table and said, "I saw Jensen today, my client with the gold mine at Downieville up by Grass Valley. He wants to take me on a tour of the mine."

"Maybe I'll get to see a real gold mine," I thought. I looked above my father's head at the pastel drawing of the view from my grandfather's cabin, waiting to hear more. My father dabbed butter on his baked potato and said, "He asked me to bring my son. Do you want to go see a gold mine, Tom?"

I dropped my fork and said, "Aren't you going to take me? I'm the one who wants to be a geologist."

"Can't do it. Miners think it's bad luck if a woman goes into a mine. Anyway, it's the sort of thing a boy does with his father. Tom would you like to go?"

Tom looked up, his gray eyes surprised, and said, "Yeah, sure," but he kept on poking little holes in his potato. My father began to tell him about the trip, emphasizing the machinery they would see.

"Daddy, why can't I go. I could dress up as a boy."

"You couldn't go into the men's bathroom and anyway Jensen knows I have only one son because he asked. Now stop arguing."

Not being allowed to go was disappointing, but feeling that my father hadn't really listened to me was worse. If women couldn't enter mines, could they still work as geologists? Mines were where the beautiful crystals were found.

I envied Tom when he came back with sparkly pieces of gold ore. They brought me one but it was small and not the same as finding it myself. I tried to get Tom to tell me about the mine but all he talked about were the hoists, the little underground railroad, and how hot it was. I couldn't visualize being in the mine.

When I started high school in the sprawling red-tile roofed building across El Camino from the Stanford stadium, I didn't think about a future career. I just thought about trying to fit in. Most girls wore cashmere sweaters in winter, but my mother said, "35 dollars for a sweater. That's ridiculous."

I was sure everyone could tell my sweaters weren't cashmere. Fashionable girls curled their hair in pin curls every night. On me pin curls just emphasized my round face. Also my girlfriends had dates, but no one ever asked me out. I thought saying hello to boys would help my datelessness, so I started keeping a chart. Once I said hello to ten boys in a day. But talk to them? No way; I was too scared. When I heard the announcement about a Sadie Hawkins girl-ask-boy dance, I decided to invite someone. I waited until an evening when my parents weren't home. Then I shut the three doors to the hallway where the black rotary phone sat in an alcove built into the wall. Just above it hung a little red and white calendar advertising the Roller and Hapgood funeral parlor. I called up three different boys and each time said, "Hello Carl (or whoever) this is Margaret Cathcart. Would you like to go to the Sadie Hawkins Dance with me?"

"Uh, no. We are going to be out of town that weekend." That was the smoothest reply. The second boy just said "No" and hung up. After the third one turned me down I felt sick and like I had a fever. When I took my temperature, it was 101. Next morning I felt fine except for the heavy lump of rejection in my stomach. This experience, repeated the next year, gave me a phobia of telephones and of inviting people that I still have.

In high school I began to think I'd like to be a forest ranger instead of a geologist. That would let me work outdoors in the mountains. Maybe I could give programs on wildflowers, trees, mountains and animals. So when our high school had a career day I signed up with Claire and Sharlene from my elementary school class to go to the program on forestry. They didn't have geology or I would have gone to that. We three were the first ones there.

The young ranger in his uniform with its scissor-edged creases asked, "What are you doing here?"

He looked as surprised as if a tree had started to talk. " Someone must have made a mistake. Girls can't be forest rangers. Don't you know that?"

Red in the face, I looked down at my white buck shoes and started walking out with Sharlene and Claire following me. "Stop. You can't do that. No one can just walk around in the halls. You have to be in a class."

We had to stay and listen to his talk even if we could never be rangers. It seemed so unfair that some men in the government had decided women couldn't be rangers. It would be 20 years before any women would be allowed to serve as rangers even in the summers. And in Idaho, Katy Breckenridge and her sister served as summer rangers at Redfish Lake in the 1970s. The uniforms they were required to wear were so unfashionable that cutting several inches off the skirts didn't do much good. It would be 40 years before I interviewed a young woman ranger on Idaho's Boise National Forest who was allowed to bring her baby to work at the ranger station.

When I went to college at Stanford, I started out majoring in geology, but it was embarrassing to be the only girl in the classes. The guys didn't speak to me and when I asked one a question about that day's lecture he said, "It's in the book", and walked away. Others pretended they didn't hear me.

In the spring of my freshman year I went to see my advisor to help me decide whether or not to keep majoring in geology. I wanted to find out more about what jobs I could get as a geologist after I graduated. My advisor was Charles Parks, the head of the geology department. Years later John McPhee would write about Parks in *Encounters With the Archdruid*. In it David Brower met three of his ideological enemies, and the first was Parks, who believed wild land should be mined or drilled regardless of its beauty or wildlife.

Parks leaned back in his swivel chair and regarded me from under semi-circular eyebrows as though I were one of the rocks on his bookcase. In my plaid cotton skirt and sleeveless white blouse, I perched on the hard oak chair, trying to look studious. A blister from my new black flats stung one heel. Running his fingers through the tumbled formation of hair at the back of his bald spot, Dr. Parks said, "You still want to be a geology major? There's a problem. Companies rarely hire women as geologists. The only opportunity for women is as paleontologists, as curators of museums. Then, too, the summer field trip is required for graduation and Stanford doesn't allow women on the field trips. As you may know, we have only one woman geology major at present, and we're trying to figure out how she can do the required work without going on the field trip."

I wasn't happy with the idea of being shut indoors with dusty fossils. Two years before my father had gotten me a part time job with a paleontology professor picking fossils out of rocks. Picking sandstone out the hinges of fossil mollusks with a needle had been frustrating. because the hinges usually broke by the time I had gotten enough sandstone out of them to be useful for the professor so I had quit. This work had made me want to be anything but a paleontologist.

As I left the building after the interview I glanced at the curled ammonites in a display case and resolved never to be shut indoors with them. It would be like being tied up in a cave. I decided to stick with the major anyway because geology had so many interesting problems, such as why minerals formed crystals when they cooled and why Africa and South America on a map looked as though they must have once been stuck together. By the following year I began to think of majoring in biology instead because I loved the mountain wildflowers, trees, and animals like the pika and mountain goat.

One Sunday during the fall of my freshman year, a friend asked me to go with her on a practice climb with the Alpine Club. The climb was at Hunters Hill near Napa northeast of San Francisco. The hill was a huge block of brown rock, perhaps 150 feet high with smaller brown blocks below it. They were surrounded by dry grass, small oak trees, and clicking grasshoppers. We beginners practiced on the smaller blocks. It was fun to learn how to climb with ropes and pitons, although I was dropped 20 feet one time when my belayer was supposed to give me slack. I wasn't hurt, just surprised, and it made my backbone tingle, but I didn't let it stop me.

During those first few weeks of college I tried out for Rally Com because I had always been fascinated by the card stunts at football games and wanted to help create them. I didn't like having to wear a tight white sweater and skirt to the games and wave pom poms but I was willing to do it to be able to help plan the card stunts.

One day while walking between classes, I mentioned the Alpine Club practice climbs to a couple of Rally Com girls. We walked beside the sandstone walls of the courtyard called the Quad. One of the girls said, "I don't know if you want to be in that club. Alpine Club girls are weird." The girl who spoke wore a low-necked Lantz dress of flowered calico trimmed with narrow ricrac. Her hair was long with the ends turned under. I envied her copper-streaked wavy hair, her dusting of freckles, her narrow waist and her expensive dress. I wished I was like her, beautiful and confident.

The girl with her wore a short-sleeved cashmere sweater, and nylons with her purple shoes. She said, "You know those girls wear dirty old jeans to class and they go camping with boys and sleep in the same tents. They have bad reputations."

That day because of what the girls said I walked right by the Alpine Club members eating their sack lunches in the courtyard of the student union. I carried my lunch past them into the off-campus students clubhouse. I worried that other students on Rally Com would find out I belonged to the Alpine Club so in the spring I didn't go have my picture taken with the Alpine Club for the yearbook. I still went on the practice climbs but I just had to fit in at Stanford or I would end up like Aunt Nellie, never getting married.

Doug as toddler on Margaret's back on way to Bench Lakes in 1957.

CHAPTER 5: IDAHO AND THE SAWTOOTHS

My husband Wayne, our son, Doug, who was then 14 months old and I moved to Idaho in June 1957 with an eight-foot U-haul trailer. Wayne had just graduated from law school and found a job in Boise.

I had met Wayne in the summer of 1953 when I worked at the new Stanford Sierra Camp at Fallen Leaf Lake. That summer he was working at American Can Company in San Jose. He had come up to visit Lada, a girl he was dating. He stayed with the family of the alumni director, Jack Shoup. Shoup was helping my father set up a non-profit to run Fallen Leaf Lodge as a camp for Stanford alumni. They were doing this to prevent the lodge from being sold to a commercial developer. Wayne knew the Shoups because he was renting a cottage in their backyard at Stanford.

I met Wayne when he came to the boat dock to find Lada. She was out in a rowboat with me and another girl. The next day when I asked Mrs. Shoup if I could borrow her car to go to Tahoe to meet a friend's bus Wayne volunteered to drive me over. He drove so fast on the one-lane road it scared me but it made me remember him. Back on campus when he saw me he would stop and talk and eventually asked me to go to a movie in Palo Alto.

Wayne was unusual because he had started the Political Union, a student organization that arranged for political figures from both parties to speak on-campus. The university hadn't previously allowed any political speakers. That made me think he was going to be elected to something someday. Wayne had been born in Buhl, Idaho, near Twin Falls, the 8th of 9 children. Even though his father owned a lumberyard, I didn't see how he had managed to go to Stanford. He was putting himself through with scholarships, summer earnings, and hashing (waiting tables) in one of the so-called Eating Clubs. He had thought of going to Stanford when he saw its poster at his high school. The poster said it offered scholarships.

When Wayne graduated from law school, his best job offer was in Boise. When he decided to accept it he said, "I was born and raised in Idaho so people know me. Idaho has less than a million people, so it won't take much money to run for Congress or the Senate."

Although I didn't like leaving all my family and friends, I was excited about the move because I thought Idaho was mostly mountains. I didn't yet know that much of the state was farms and sagebrush and that the culture was different from California's. I also didn't realize it took more than one day to drive the 650 miles from Palo Alto to Boise.

On a hundred-degree morning we loaded the trailer in my parents' driveway in Palo Alto. We put in Doug's crib and high chair, my desk, an old oak dresser, our clothes and boxes of books. Our things were in my parents garage because we had given up our apartment to house sit for my Grandma Edna that spring while she went to Europe. My parents house was long and narrow and painted white with rooms over an attached garage at one end. It stood next to an alley where a big Monterey pine grew and gave the street its name.

My father had said goodbye the night before, because he commuted by train to San Francesco. Just as Wayne and I finished loading, my mother stepped into the garage, rubbing her hands on her flowered apron. Her white-sprinkled hair stood up in a wiry tuft. She pointed to a pile of boxes on the dusty floor. "You need to take your rock collection. We don't have space. If you don't take it I'm going to give it to Goodwill."

Wayne slammed the trailer doors, his scalp shining through his crew cut in the hot sun. I shuddered at the noise. "Wayne, I've got to take my rocks. She's going to throw them away. I've spent hundreds of hours on them."

Wayne shook his head. "You don't need those rocks. You don't do anything with them. We'll never get the trailer to Idaho with them in it."

"Please, If I don't take my rocks I would leave part of myself behind."

"You ll regret it. They'll just be in the way."

"Oh," I said, and walked around the garage to the back lawn to hide my tears. I stared at the white boards of the garage. If I kept the rocks, maybe I could still someday go back to college and be a geologist. Many of the rocks were pieces of mountains I had climbed, pieces of my life.

Then I felt Wayne's arms around me. "If they mean that much to you, we'll take them," he said. He helped me load the five big cartons. As we put Doug into his car seat and prepared to drive away, my mother came out to the trailer, sniffing into her handkerchief. Her eyes were red. I couldn't see why she was crying. I was only moving away, having an adventure, not dying. I had no idea what the move would mean to me, but she did because she had grown up in upper New York State and had left there forever when she married. She had seen her parents only once in the first five years.

A couple of hours into our trip we drove past the windmills and apricot orchards of the central valley. Our car was a small Willys sedan. Doug's car seat was attached only by metal loops wedged under the front seat's back.

Because of the trailer we did not take the main road over Donner Pass. Instead we drove my dad's route on back roads to US 50 and on it over Echo Summit and around the south end of Lake Tahoe. Near Placerville, the narrow curving road met another at a stop sign on a hill. Here the engine died. When Wayne started the car again, it wouldn't shift out of low gear. Hitting the steering wheel with his fist, he said, "The trailer's too heavy. Why did you make me take your rocks?"

As Wayne drove on, the radiator began to bubble and steam poured out. When the ground flattened, he stopped and waited for the radiator to cool enough to add water. We crept on to Placerville, then spent the rest of the day in a motel while the clutch was replaced. Wayne slept, but Doug was wide awake so I had to stay up.

In late afternoon, we started over the Sierra. Among pine trees less than 20 miles beyond Placerville the car boiled over again. We pulled off and waited three hours for the sun to set. Wayne read and I looked at picture books with Doug. His white-blonde hair stuck to his scalp with sweat. Time seemed tethered above us in one place like a kite.

It took all night to drive the narrow winding road over Echo Summit, and descend to Lake Tahoe. Beyond it we drove over Spooner Summit to Carson City. When we drove past the turnoff to Fallen Leaf near the village of Myers I realized I was leaving Fallen Leaf. I would rarely see its pink and white heather and glacier sculptured granite, again. At breakfast in Carson City I could eat only half a pancake. Next we drove on out into the Nevada desert. Doug kept pointing out the car window, saying, "Daw! Doggie!" at the sagebrush.

Soon the car began boiling again, so we spent the day at a motel in Lovelock waiting for evening. While Wayne slept, I wheeled Doug in his stroller to the city park to play on the swings and slides.

As we drove on that night, so many jackrabbits bounded back and forth Wayne couldn't avoid hitting them. With each thump I worried we'd go off the road. Two or three larger thumps were probably coyotes. As the sun rose, we neared the Idaho border among sagebrush and brown outcrops. There we picked up a trucker beside a broken-down truck full of tomatoes. He handed us a box of tomatoes for our trouble. "They're all going to spoil anyway."

At the top of the grade above the Boise Valley, the trucker insisted we stop to look at the view. A quilt of green squares and rectangles spread out between the dust-brown hills and timber-topped mountains across the valley. The trucker waved his hairy hand. "Doesn't that look like the Garden of Eden?"

After our three-day struggle with the boiling car and no sleep, it did. The following day we looked for a place to rent. The best we could find was a little two-story house next to the Union Pacific depot. Every passing train shook the house and rattled the windows.

From our upstairs window we looked across Boise to golden velvet foothills, and wooded ridges. The valley below them held pastures, barns, cottonwoods and the blue curves of the Boise River. I liked the apartment and its view, but the trains scared Doug. During the day he'd climb into my lap. If he was in his crib when one came by, he got up on his hands and knees and banged his head on the headboard. I wondered if he was pretending to be a train to scare the noise away.

From the depot gardens next door we could look down Capitol Boulevard to the white dome of the state capitol. I was disappointed not to be right next to the mountains, and more disappointed to find the nearby mountains had no trails, only rough dirt roads. Those roads except for the road to the Bogus Basin ski area were best driven in a 4-wheel drive pickup, which we didn't have.

Two weeks after we moved to Boise, we drove 125 miles to Buhl for a Fourth of July picnic in Wayne's parent's backyard. The backyard was enclosed by a white picket fence and shaded by a big cottonwood tree. It also contained a vegetable garden and a clothesline with five long wires. The ham, fried chicken, potato salad and Jello was served on a wooden picnic table and most of us sat on the grass. After the noon picnic most of us drove down to Slager's hot springs pool at Thousand Springs on the Snake River.

The gathering included four of Wayne's six sisters, his two brothers, the husbands of two of the sisters, and a dozen children. The oldest sister, Marjorie, had eight. The front, back, and side of the little gray house had glassed-in porches, making it look as though the whole first floor was made of little panes of glass. The house had one bedroom on the main floor and one in the attic, and there was only one bath. For a time Wayne's bedroom had been a 6 by 8 foot closet off the attic bedroom. Later he shared the unheated, side porch with his brothers. His six older sisters had all graduated from college or nursing school. His older brother was working at the lumber yard and the younger was going to Colorado State college.

I had met Wayne's relatives except for his sister Doris and her children on our visit two years before. Their friendliness had made me feel right at home, although they talked in Idaho accents with broad A's and the subjects were all local. No one talked about world events the way my family did.

During the 4th of July the phone kept ringing for Wayne's father, and he kept going down to the lumberyard to sell the callers lumber, nails, paint, stepladders, etc.

I asked Wayne's mother how she had ever raised nine children. With a droll smile on her round face, she said, "I didn't get them all at once." She laughed, the tight curls of her permed gray hair bouncing. "Seriously, one of the ways I did it was to keep my cellar full. Would you like to see it?"

She asked Wayne to lift up the cellar door, a slanting door in the back porch floor. She picked up a flashlight, said "Watch your heads," and led us down steep steps onto the dirt floor of the earthen-walled cellar. Her head just cleared the joists so Wayne and I had to stoop. "There," she said proudly, "I can everything I can get hold of - - cherries, chickens, beans, tomatoes, corn."

On wooden shelves, hundreds of jars glowed with red, green, orange, or purple in the dim light. Some of the shelves held tin cans marked in black crayon with numbers and letters like Ck-57 and Co-56. "I go to the cannery in Twin for things like chicken and string beans." She told me that this cannery was open to anyone who had things to can. The person did the labor of filling the cans and the cannery provided the cans and the processing at a high temperature for a price per can.

"I don't know how to can," I said, "but I've made jam."

"It's not that much harder." Back upstairs she sat me down at her kitchen table and showed me how to can in glass jars using a giant enamel kettle to boil them in.

When we went home, I bought a charcoal-gray enamel canner, mason jars and lids, and canned some apricots and cherries. I had already learned from women at the Welcome Wagon club meetings that Idaho women did a lot of canning. I wanted to have something in common with the women I met. I didn't tell anyone that the lids of several of my jars refused to seal, so I had to keep them in the refrigerator until we ate the contents.

Three weeks after our visit to Buhl, I spent a Saturday dusting the furniture, scrubbing the bathrooms, mopping the floors, washing the windows and sweeping the walks. I even washed Doug's toy truck. My parents and my18-year old sister Dodie were arriving for a visit the next evening. I couldn't wait to see them.

In the paper the next morning I was horrified to see a little article about the deaths of two daughters of a Stanford professor. My Fallen Leaf friend Margaret Brown and her sister Carrie had been killed the day before in a wreck on the eastern side of the Sierras. Why hadn't my parents called if it were true? "No, no, it can't be," I said, bursting into tears. Wayne got up from the Formica-topped table in his striped bathrobe, came over and hugged me from behind my chair. "What's the matter?"

I pointed to the article. A train churned by outside. Wayne rubbed my shoulder and said, "I don't think it's the same people. They probably got it wrong. Brown is a common name."

If it really was our Browns, my parents wouldn't be coming. They must have forgotten they planned to drive to Idaho and never thought of calling us.

I thought about the Browns all day while I cooked and straightened up the house in case my parents came after all. They finally arrived in late evening. In the porch light their faces drooped like deflated balloons. Dodie climbed out of the car like an old person, still wearing her dark glasses. Carrie had been her best friend, and had just graduated from high school with her. I asked why they hadn't called to let us know about the Browns.

"We wanted to tell you in person and we didn't think there would be anything in your paper because Idaho is so far away," my mother said in a croaky voice. "We came up here instead of going to the funeral," she sniffed. "I only have this week off, so if we didn't come we wouldn't get to see Douggie for a whole year. I couldn't bear that."

That evening we heard more. My parents and Dodie and her friend Carrie had just spent a week hiking some of the Yosemite High Sierra camps. On their trip they had visited Margaret who was working at the Vogelsang camp and took Margaret back with them for a short visit with her parents. When Margaret got a ride back with another employee she took Carrie with her because there was an opening for her to work at Vogelsang. "If we hadn't given them a ride to Fallen Leaf they'd still be alive," my mother said. I had no idea how to comfort her or Dodie or myself. To me, living so far away, it felt as though Fallen Leaf itself had died.

When my parents and Dodie left after three days I mourned the loss of Fallen Leaf as well as that of Margaret and Carrie. To keep from thinking too much I tried to accomplish as many things as possible each day. I made lists and crossed off the tasks as I finished them. I sewed with the used sewing machine my father had bought me for $50 during his visit. The waist on the first dress I made came out too short and I had to redo it. I canned peaches and at the local cannery, applesauce and corn. Wayne's mother sent the corn from Wayne's sister Marjorie's farm on the Greyhound bus. In those days, Greyhound operated a package service similar to UPS except that you had to go down to the bus station to send and get the packages. I worked on the correspondence art course I had signed up for the winter before. I met a few women my age in the Welcome Wagon Newcomers Club and in Julia Davis Park when I took Doug there to play.

I wanted to go camping in the Idaho mountains as Fallen Leaf receded into the past. It took on a magical light and I longed to go to the Idaho mountains as a substitute. That longing increased when I saw huge black and white photographs of the Sawtooths in Falk's ID department store downtown. The Sawtooths weren't just the forested hills I had seen on our honeymoon two years before when forest fire smoke had hidden their cliffs and towers.

I had been so determined to go hiking that summer that in the spring I had bought a little pack frame, thinking Doug could sit on its shelf, and I could tie him onto it. I had already discovered that the wheels of his stroller wouldn't go up the dirt roads near our apartment back in Stanford. The pack frame would make it easier to carry Doug, if I could persuade Wayne to go to the mountains.

In mid-August when it got to be over 100 degrees, Wayne finally agreed to take the weekend off from studying for the bar exam and go camping. We went to the Sawtooths because of the pictures in the ID store and because Wayne had hiked and camped there when he was a boy scout. To save on gas we drove the shortest distance on the map, which was along unpaved roads between Idaho City and Stanley. The roads were so narrow and bumpy we got only half way, and camped in Bear Valley that Friday evening. We laid out the navy-surplus life raft sail that was our ground cloth and put our sleeping bags on top of it. Wayne set the food box and our rusty green ice chest on the rickety picnic table. Doug wandered around, picking up pebbles and trying to eat them. He wore a blue nylon jacket and red woolly hat with little white dogs on it that my mother had given him.

At bedtime I was worried Doug would get up and wander while we were asleep, so I zipped him into his snowsuit, wrapped him in his blankie, and put him in the car. He soon fell asleep, but a couple of hours later woke, cold and frightened. Wayne took him out of the car and squeezed him into his own sleeping bag, which had just enough room because it was an old style rectangular bag.

Next morning, we continued on the bumpy dirt road through meadows of pale purple wildflowers. After a couple of hours we were driving beneath the jagged mountain wall of the Sawtooths.

At Stanley, we stopped at the log hotel for a second breakfast of pancakes. The town had only three streets, all of them dirt. The roads that led east to Challis and south to Ketchum weren't then paved. Beside Stanley the Salmon River wound in white rapids, and green pools that also reflected the blue sky.

On the hotel menu, I read that prospectors from Idaho City had discovered the area and named it the Stanley Basin for the oldest member of their party, Captain

John Stanley. As miners came to the surrounding mountains in the 1870s, one of them, Arthur McGown, built a supply station here. Gradually two villages had grown up around it, upper and lower Stanley.

From Stanley we drove south five miles and then two miles west to Redfish Lake. The road led toward a tall mountain with a fan of cliffs and gullies. I saw a sign, Bench Lakes 3. A trail! We could go on a hike!

After buying milk at the little store, we found a campsite at the only campground, which was called The Point. On a little hill, we spread out our sleeping bags on our navy life raft sail, put the cooking pots on the picnic table, Then we carried Doug down through low bushes to a wide beach. A breeze rippled the water and brought the smells of pine and fir. Above a wooded ridge on the right, rose the towers and chimneys of the big mountain Wayne said was Mt. Heyburn. Across the lake, triangles of rock gathered into another dramatic mountain. At the head of the lake, a U-shaped canyon separated the two peaks. It looked much like the view of Cathedral Peak, Tallac, and the Angoras from the lower end of Fallen Leaf. I had only been to that end once, because there was then no road to it then. The resemblance of Redfish to Fallen Leaf was uncanny.

That evening as Wayne stood at the picnic table in his black and orange letter sweater helping wash dishes, I asked him if we could hike to Bench Lakes the next day. Doug sat in his stroller, sucking his thumb and rubbing his grimy yellow blanket against his cheek. "We have to drive home tomorrow. I have to work Monday." Wayne replied, nesting cups into the cook set.

I sighed and thought we'd have to wait until the next summer. The next morning while Wayne was filling our kettle at the pump, another camper told him about a shortcut to Bench Lakes that saved a mile. Wayne loved shortcuts, and if the hike was only 2 miles we could surely do it by noon and still have time to drive home,

With three old belts I buckled Doug onto the canvas shelf of the little pack frame. The frame was made of aluminum tubing bent into two rectangles that fitted together at a 90 degree angle. It was covered with army green canvas, Webbing shoulder straps were attached to the top and bottom. Wayne carried the pack frame with Doug and. I carried a knapsack containing our lunch and Wayne's fishing gear. We started up the steep pine-needle-covered slope in back of the campground. I felt like a helium balloon. I was so happy to be going on a hike for the first time in two years, but the steep slope was slow going.

After we'd climbed a few yards, Doug began to slide off the shelf of the pack frame. We had to stop and lift him back on and tighten the belts. After an extremely steep half mile of pine needles with no trail, we came to the main trail. Once we were on its much gentler grade, Doug stopped sliding off. Squinting and blinking in the sunlight, he looked all around, chewed the sticks I gave him to play with, and beat them on his knees. After a couple of miles, a trail turned off up a ridge to the right at a sign for the Sawtooth Primitive Area.

In a steep half mile from the sign, we reached the first lake, but there was no shade so we continued a few yards into the trees and found a second lake. It was so close to Mt. Heyburn that we could see the tiny teeth on its towers.

After lunch, Wayne walked around to the other side of the lake to fish. Doug played in the V between two big logs, while I sat at their open end. He kept trying to climb out of the log enclosure, and when he squeezed past me, he said, “I go way.”

I grinned. It was his first sentence and he said it on a hike! Later, as we plodded back to the car through the brush and pines, my face was stiff with sunburn but I felt a deep contentment. I vowed to return as often as possible to these new mountains.

Working on the cabin foundations.

CHAPTER 6: BUILDING OUR CABIN

We moved to Caldwell, 25 miles west of Boise, in December 1958. Our first daughter, Leslie, was born 2 months later, on Valentine's Day. Caldwell was out in the flat farmland much farther from the Sawtooths and far from the wooded hills above Boise. We moved because Wayne had been laid off from the law firm in Boise and after four months had found a new job as deputy prosecutor for Canyon County in Caldwell. After a few months in Caldwell renting an ancient house with a coal furnace we bought a modern two-bedroom house near the high school.

Across the street lived Chuck and Betty Banks, who went backpacking and talked a lot about their trips. They had two boys of scouting age. Betty kept telling me about backpacking in the Sawtooths to Alice and Toxaway Lakes and some mystery lakes they called Shangri-la. And after they and the scout troop rafted the Middle Fork of the Salmon they invited us over to see a movie of the trip. I remember this was before a road was built to Dagger Falls at Boundary Creek where today's rafters start. The scouts and their leaders drove rough roads from Cascade and Warm Lake to the upper end of Pistol Creek, a tributary of the Middle Fork. From there they hiked down to the river. They had horses or mules, perhaps belonging to friends, carrying the rafts and food and gear down to the river. I don't remember how far down the river they floated, maybe only a couple of days to the Indian Creek guard station. I was fascinated by that trip and looked forward to going backpacking or rafting in the Idaho mountains sometime myself.

Hearing about the neighbors trips made Wayne's spending his vacations at Army Reserve summer camps even more difficult for me than it would have done otherwise. It meant that he had no vacation time for taking me and the kids to the mountains. More than once I asked him to quit the Reserve, but he just said, "We need the extra money." Years later I figured out that he had a strong wish to serve in the military as five of his six older sisters had done in World War II and Korea. I think he felt it was part of his family tradition as well as being a patriotic thing to do,

In addition to hearing about Betty and Chuck's trips my mother's weekly letters told about the hikes my parents and my brother and sister went on and I envied them. When Wayne was at camp I sometimes went to Fallen Leaf if my parents' vacations were at the same time. My parents paid for a plane ticket to Reno for me and Doug once and bus tickets for Doug and Leslie and me once. These trips let me do some hiking with my dad and neighbors while my mother babysat. But it wasn't the same as being able to hike with Wayne.

When my parents weren't at Fallen Leaf during Wayne's camp, the two weeks of 100 degree heat at home seemed like forever. No women I knew took their kids camping without their husbands and none of my friends were the least bit interested in going with me. I was too scared of bears and mountain lions and rushing creeks to camp with the kids by myself. Wayne and I went on one or two weekend camping trips with the kids each summer, but it was so hard to tent camp with toddlers it wasn't any fun.

I especially remember camping at Cascade Lake with some friends and their twins who were Doug's age. Leslie was 18 months old. As soon as we set her down at the campsite, she picked up and tried to eat every pebble, which of course would choke her if we didn't take them away. The first evening mosquitoes covered her with red, itchy bites in spite of bug repellant. We couldn't take our travel crib because there was no mattress to belt it to, and we didn't think to take the playpen. So getting her to take a nap was impossible, and getting her to sleep at night took hours. Wayne was angry at me that I had not kept her from getting bitten, and said he'd never go camping again.

On my trips to Fallen Leaf it was so much easier to stay in my grandfather's cabin than it had been to go camping with the kids and Wayne that I wished we had a cabin of our own in Idaho. At Grandpa's cabin we slept in beds or army cots and walked floors instead of pebbles and pine cones. The cabin had electric lights and a flush toilet that was only 50 feet from the bunkhouse. Doors kept the kids from wandering off. There were no nearby creeks and the lake was a quarter mile away.

In the spring of 1961 I read in the *Idaho Statesman* that the Sawtooth National Forest was leasing cabin sites near Alturas Lake in the Sawtooths. The leases, which they called permits, cost only $40 a year. I was so excited and I showed Wayne the article and said I think we should look for a lot.

Wayne looked up from the sports section, pushed back a lock of his reddish brown hair and said, "It is too soon to look. We won't be able to build a cabin for a long time."

"Can't we go look at the lots anyway?"

"I guess we can look if I don't have to promise to get one."

That Labor Day weekend we drove up to the Sawtooths to look at the lots. On the way we left Doug with Wayne's mother ln Buhl because he had just had his tonsils out and the doctor had said he couldn't go to a higher altitude yet. We took two-year-old Leslie with us. We drove to Ketchum next to Sun Valley, and over Galena Summit to the headwaters of the Salmon River. The 40 miles of road from Ketchum over Galena Summit to the turnoff to Alturas Lake then was just gravel and dirt except for a paved section over the summit. From the head of the valley we drove through sagebrush and pastures to the Sawtooth Valley Ranger Station. It stood on green lawns below sagebrush hills. Behind the hills rose peaks of startling white rock. Across the valley and river the teeth of the Sawtooths cut into a sky so deep a blue it was purple. I sat on the lawn beside our pale green Ford station wagon, where Leslie was asleep. I savored the tang of the sagebrush and the damp smell of the river. In the valley I noticed an airstrip and a network of power lines and wondered how soon the valley would be full of houses. When Wayne came out of the ranger station, he had a map of the cabin area with the lots that were taken crossed out.

The road to the cabins sites ran through sagebrush, crossed a creek under lodgepole pines, and then went through meadows surrounded by a Douglas fir forest. On the road were several fir cones with what looked like little tails coming out of their scales. Along the road were currant bushes with berries like red glass beads. Above the high point in the loop road was Lot 31 and I liked it the best of the sites we saw. At the back of it grew 200-foot Douglas firs. Across the valley to the east rose white and pinkish gray peaks. While we were looking at the lot Leslie stayed asleep in the car. Before we decided on a lot, Wayne said, "I want to go look at the lots on the private land at Alturas Lake before we decide. They are only $750."

Those lots were condemned by the Forest Service many years ago.

We drove over there and looked but found all the lodgepoles on these lots covered with dust from the dirt road. So we went back to the ranger station where Wayne wrote a check for the $40 and filled out an application for Lot 31 on the top of the knoll.

On Labor Day weekend the next year we went from a family gathering at Buhl up to measure the distance between the Douglas firs . We checked those distances with plans we had bought from a house plan book. Luckily, the cabin in the plans would fit between the trees. Wayne, Doug, Leslie, our third child Neal, who was then only 3 months old, and I stayed upstairs in the old Alturas Lake Lodge, which is not there anymore. About 1970 the Forest Service cut the building in half, moved the pieces out into the valley near Smiley Creek Lodge, and sold them for giant cabins. They are still there, looking historic and dilapidated.

On the 1962 trip we went back to the ranger station and submitted the cabin plans to the ranger, Ralph Cisco, Then we drove home by way of Fairfield which is between Hailey and Mountain Home even though that road then was still just dirt. We wanted to see if it was faster than going through Shoshone. It was much slower. Today's road between Lowman and Stanley, the one we usually take, hadn't been built yet.

While waiting for the cabin to be built during the next few years, I read about Senator Frank Church s proposal for a national park in the Sawtooths. I also saw an account of a couple's trip to lakes in the White Clouds called the Boulder Chain. There were so many of these lakes and they were so remote they didn't have individual names, just numbers. The article made my legs tingle. I so much wanted to hike to them.

In the spring of 1963 the Forest Service sent us a letter reminding us that the permit required that we build a cabin within two years. I was glad they sent the letter because it meant that Wayne couldn't put off building the cabin. We couldn't get a mortgage for a cabin because we already had one on our house, and in those days banks were strict about mortgages. However we could buy the materials from the lumberyard Wayne's father had started that was then run by his two brothers.

Wayne persuaded a client, Lou Gepford, who was a carpenter, to help him. They started on the foundations on the 4th of July weekend. I had thought I could camp on the lot with the kids, but Wayne said, "If you want us to get anything done you better stay home."

In July Wayne and Mr. Gepford spent two or three weekends digging trenches, building forms, and mixing and pouring cement by hand for the footings. I hadn't known that builders had to put in footings before they built the foundations. I learned that footings are cement poured into trenches on which the foundations are constructed.

The Rural Electrification Association was bringing in power lines to the cabin area that summer. They had installed a power pole on our lot with an electrical outlet on it. For $40 Wayne got a REA worker to flatten the top of the knoll and scrape out a semicircular driveway. While working there, Wayne and Mr, Gepford camped out in our umbrella tent. Because the ground behind the cabin sloped, they both ended up on the lower side of the tent every morning.

The kids and I stayed home but three weeks later I drove the kids to Fallen Leaf while Wayne went to army reserve camp. I was able to do some hiking with my parents and cabin neighbors, while I carried Neal in a baby backpack. We had bought it to carry Leslie when she was a baby. It was called a Hikeapoose. On Labor Day weekend the kids and I went to the cabin site and watched Wayne and his brother Bruce put up a second row of cinder blocks for the foundation. Then Doug and Leslie laid boards on top of the cinder blocks and weighted them down with rocks to keep out the snow. Neal watched from his wooden playpen, sucking his middle finger and rubbing his cheek with his yellow blanket.

I thought the cabin would soon be finished, but I was wrong. It would take five more years before it was built and 24 years after that before it was finished. Things kept interfering with saving enough money and Wayne having enough time to build even the walls and roof.

First, when Doug started school we needed a house with more than one bathroom so both Wayne and Doug could get ready on time in the mornings. The basement floor was lower than the sewer out in the street so we couldn't put a bathroom in the basement. That meant we needed a different house. Choices were poor in our price range, so we had a house built in 1964. It was two stories plus an unfinished basement. That was the kind of design that gave us the most square feet for the money.

Then Wayne and his law partner had the opportunity to go in with an optometrist to build an office building. That building was constructed in 1967 and the law firm moved into it in February 1968. We also had two more children, Hilary in 1965 and Stuart in 1967. As far as Wayne's time went he was elected chairman of the Canyon County Democrats in 1966.

But every year we drove up to check on the cabin foundations. One year we had a flat tire on our trip and stopped to get it fixed at Trigger Jim's at Obsidian, eight miles north of the cabin turnoff. While there we met JG Nicholson, the mayor of Stanley who ran a laundromat and did construction. Wayne talked to him about helping build our cabin and he said he would like to do that.

While the tire was being patched that day, Jim Decker showed the kids and me his ice house where he stored salmon for fishermen on sawdust-covered blocks of ice. He cut the ice on Alturas Lake in the winter. Some of the salmon he showed us were three feet long. Decker was the postmaster for the village of Obsidian. The post office was an eight by ten plywood shack, painted white, that stood beside the cafe. Decker told us that if we walked up the hill behind the cafe, we might find some of the obsidian for which the place was named, but the tire was ready, so we didn't go look then. Obsidian is a black volcanic glass that the Indians often used for arrowheads,

In the winter of 1968, we received another letter from the Forest Service. It said if we didn't complete our cabin in two more years they would revoke our permit. We both felt we could not let this happen. After we received the letter Wayne and I sat at our maple dining table going over the mail. Now and then we heard the kids feet thumping from upstairs.

Wayne picked up the Forest Service letter and looked at me through his gold-rimmed glasses. He said, "I don't think the Forest Service will cancel the lease but if they do well just look for some private land."

“Please build the cabin. I’ll be finished getting my teaching credential in a couple of years and then we’ll have plenty of money for it.”

“We can’t afford to do it now, even if I do all the work myself and I don’t have enough time anyway.”

“You would if you quit Army Reserve.”

“We need the money I get from reserve if we’re ever going to build the cabin.”

“The kids are going to be all grown up before we build it, and we never get to have family vacations.”

“Bullshit!” Wayne slammed the table. “We had a vacation when you went to Fort Lewis with me and you and the kids stayed at Letty’s and I’ve taken you to Fallen Leaf several times.”

With a choking voice I said, “It’s not the same. You always use most of your vacation for Reserve.”

I bit my lip and ran upstairs.

A couple of months later Wayne must have thought more about how soon the kids would be all grown up. Doug would be going off to college in only six more years. Wayne decided to quit reserve so he would have the time to build the cabin. He hired Mr. Nicholson from Stanley and spent three weeks with him, building the plywood shell of the cabin. Doug, who was then 12, helped for two of the weeks, after he returned from scout camp. They stayed in a little camping trailer belonging to Wayne’s brother, Bruce, and drove home to rest each weekend. As he and Doug were leaving for the third week, Wayne said the kids and I could come up and see the cabin as soon as they finished the work if the kids were good.

I had an exhausting time while they were gone. My brother Tom, his wife Debbie, and two year old daughter Amy visited, and Wayne’s mother dropped in with four of her grandchildren one day without calling first. Also that spring after Bobby Kennedy and Martin Luther King were assassinated, our church had undertaken a project to bring children from the Robert Taylor Homes in Chicago for a month’s visit in Caldwell. We had signed up to take a child, not realizing the month would coincide with the weeks that Mr. Nicholson and Wayne planned to build the cabin. So I had extra things to do to entertain seven year old Aafriika and take her to gatherings organized by the church.

The church project came about because the assassinations that spring had inspired a member of our congregation to do something to counteract the violence and racism in our society. Bill Crookham, of Crookham Seeds, enlisted the help of a woman in the church, Evelyn Cates, who was a social worker. She was able to arrange for church families to take in 12 children from the Robert Taylor homes (one of the Chicago projects) for a month.

One day I hired a sitter just so I could buy groceries in peace. While I was gone Leslie and Aafriika got in a fight and as I drove home, I found Aafriika walking down the street with her suitcase, She said she was going to walk back to Chicago. I persuaded her to turn around and come back to the house with me. Because she and her family moved a year later we lost track of her for many years. The internet reconnected us about four years ago and we enjoy e-mailing back and forth. She passed the licensing exam to be a physician's assistant in November. However, she has decided not to work as one because of the prejudice in the field of medicine. Instead she is in training to be a cosmetologist.

After Doug, Wayne and Mr. Nicholson had spent three weeks building, Wayne called and said, "We're finished and we're coming home."

With a gulp I said, "You told the children they could come up and see the cabin if they were good. They've been good."

The kids were happy playing with their toys, their friends and Aafriika. It was me who needed to see the cabin right away. After some discussion, Wayne agreed to stay there with Doug until we arrived.

Just getting ready to go to the cabin was a lot of work. First, I did laundry and bought groceries and disposable diapers for Stuart. Then with my help the children packed their unbleached muslin duffel bags, labeled with each one's initials, which I had sewed for them.

The next day on the way to the cabin I found it a challenge to keep the children from fighting, and to keep them in their seat belts. As sagebrush and evergreens flashed by outside the car, it seemed like directing a play in a bus.

When we arrived at the cabin site at last we saw a huge plywood box on the sagebrush knoll with thick forest behind it. The box had holes in it for future windows. No one was there when we arrived. I worried Wayne and Doug had gone home after all. It was lunch time so we got out of the car and started eating the sandwiches I had made the night before. Before we finished eating, Wayne and Doug drove up in a Fuller Farm and Home Supply truck that was full of the windows for the cabin.

Although the cabin was only partly done my heart felt as though it had climbed into the sky and I had to wipe my eyes. We entered the cabin by the back doorway because the front door was three feet above the ground for access to a future deck.

The weeks of sun had spread Doug s freckles into tan patches that matched his hair. Beaming with pride he led us on a tour of the new cabin, pointing out the cutout for the picture window in the front wall and its view. Through it we could see gray, cream and pink summits of the Boulder and White Cloud Mountains across the valley. Chipboard covered the floor and only two by fours divided the rooms. In the middle, plugged into an orange extension cord, hummed an ancient refrigerator on six-inch legs.

One at a time, Wayne guided us up the ribbed rungs of an aluminum extension ladder to see the loft that covered all the rooms except the main living area. In the loft he had outlined five little rooms for the kids with two by fours.

“That is so clever, the little rooms,” I said and hugged Wayne, feeling very lucky. It wasn’t the cabin itself, but Wayne’s effort in building it with his own hands that awed me.

“Mr. Nicholson is going to put on the siding, shingles and windows by Labor Day.”

That night the kids and I stayed in two little cabins at the lodge at Alturas Lake, which was about five miles from the cabin. The lodge was being closed down for good, so there was nothing in one of the cabins and only a bed in the other, but we managed. Wayne and Doug stayed in the camping trailer they had used while building.

For Labor Day weekend we hired a sitter for Hilary and Stuart and brought Doug, Leslie and Neal with us to help stain the cabin siding reddish brown and paint the window frames beige. Bruce and his wife Beverly drove up from Buhl to help paint. They brought an intricately carved door with them for the front door, but Wayne thought it was too beautiful for a cabin. So we took it home for our house in Caldwell. For the two nights we were there we slept on the floor in our sleeping bags.

As we left for home, after the painting the brown cabin with its tan roof reminded me of my grandfather’s cabin at Fallen Leaf. It might have a tan roof instead of green and weathered boards nailed over the windows instead of orange shutters, and around it grew way more sagebrush, but it held the future. It promised hikes with Wayne and my children just as wonderful as the ones with my parents, Tom, Dodie, my friend Margaret Brown and others when I was young. Still I worried about how many more summers I would have to stay home with the kids while Wayne worked to finish the cabin. At least it was partly done. A few days later when I talked to my brother Tom, he said, “You don’t have to finish it before you start staying in it, you know. Just take up some furniture.”

So the following June we did. Now that the cabin was up and had furniture I knew life would be much more of an adventure.

Stuart, age 3, at Sawtooth Lake when he walked all the way there.

CHAPTER 7: THE PAPER PLATE HIKES

The second summer we had the cabin, I was even more eager to hike from it than I had been the first summer. I also wanted to take a pack trip. I mentioned this to Wayne while we were up skiing at Bogus Basin one Wednesday afternoon, Wayne said he wanted to do something more relaxing like a raft trip. "Kids are not allowed, so we could have a vacation from them. It would still be in the mountains, and it would be an adventure."

"You mean a trip of several days? How can we find a babysitter for that long?"

"Look out, I need to raise the foot rest."

We were getting to the top of the chairlift. We had been able to ski on a Wednesday afternoon only once before that winter because Wayne had been so busy. Wayne was serving as chairman of the Canyon County Democrats and his law partner, Bill Brauner, was running for Congress. I loved those ski afternoons because it gave us a chance to talk away from the kids and the television. I put both poles in one hand and grabbed the side of the chair. The top was coming up fast. I gauged the right moment, set my skis down on the snow, and stood up. My skis rasped down the icy ramp to a stop. Wayne skied down beside me and stopped. The sun accented the blue ruts in the snow.

"We can work out the babysitting," he said. "There's a guy I met when I was in JayCees and he takes rafting trips on the Middle Fork."

"But I hoped we were going to take a pack trip and work on the cabin."

"I don't think so. I need any vacation to be restful, and we'd have to take the kids with us on a pack trip. That would be too much work. A river trip would be much more fun. And we still can't afford to have anything done on the cabin. I spent my money and three weeks of my vacation two years ago to build the cabin. Now it is your turn to earn the money for it."

I didn't say anything more, just shoved off and headed for Showcase, an intermediate run I liked. Sitting in boats going down a river would be a lazy way to spend a vacation, and the kids wouldn't get to spend time in the mountains.

I wasn't willing to get a regular job to earn money for the cabin because I had found the only jobs open to women like me with only a bachelor's degree were secretary, waitress, or retail clerk. When we had lived in Boise and I worked as a part time secretary for an insurance agent, more than half my salary had gone for child care. So I wouldn't even earn enough for child care because we now had five kids. Obtaining a teaching credential seemed to be the best idea. It would require me to take only a few classes. Plus, I would have summers off to go to the cabin. And I wouldn't have to start working yet. I didn't consider whether I'd enjoy teaching or be any good at it, but I decided to sign up for a class in the fall.

I worked hard around the house and Wayne didn't give me any credit for it because I wasn't earning any money. I realize now that I had little idea how the real world worked and that I had to adapt to it and also learn to be patient.

In late July we took the float trip on the Middle Fork of the Salmon River with Eldon Handy. We began the trip at the Boundary Creek launch site, just below Dagger Falls. Reaching it required a 49 mile drive north of Stanley, half that on a dirt road.

On the river we rode in big rubber rafts, which were paddled by the outfitter's staff and family. The trip began in wooded hills covered with lodgepole pine and Douglas fir. Five days later it went through the rapids, cliffs, and sagebrush of Impassable

Canyon and ended at the confluence of the Middle Fork with the main Salmon River.

There were three other lawyers on the trip so in the evenings the guys had a great time discussing cases while steaks, or chicken halves, or foil-wrapped trout sizzled on the campfire. The other male guest directed a museum in Pennsylvania and taught us several risque songs. Evidently, the river trip put Wayne in a better mood about the cabin. Later that summer he spent three days helping a plumber from Buhl put in pipes under the cabin floor for the rough plumbing.

After the raft trip, Wayne went to Warm Lake to help at the scout camp while Doug was there. While they were gone I drove to the cabin with the four younger kids. I was eager to look for the 4th of July Lake again and to see as much of the backcountry near our cabin as possible. I don't know why I thought I had to see it right away. It was just something I was eager to do and I expected my family to go along with it. Only later would I realize there are two kinds of people who enjoy being in the mountains, those obsessed with them like me and those for whom mountains are just one of many interests.

As I hiked with the kids that summer I felt guilty that I wasn't out knocking on doors for Cecil Andrus, who was running for governor. The campaign went on amid a big controversy over proposed mining in the White Clouds. The then governor, Don Samuelson, who had defeated Andrus in the preceding election, favored the mining. American Smelting Mining and Refining company (ASARCO) had found a large deposit of molybdenum on the side of the highest peak in the White Clouds, Castle Peak. Samuelson said the tailings pond they planned would be a beautiful lake, but many people were horrified by the idea. So was Andrus and he campaigned against the mine. The controversy over what to do with the Sawtooths and White Clouds had been going on since 1911 when a group of women's organizations had proposed the Sawtooths be made into a national park. By the summer of 1970 the Sawtooths were a Wilderness Area, which had been designated by the 1964 Wilderness Act but the White Clouds were still non-wilderness. Some Idahoans supported a park but most wanted to have the areas stay with the Forest Service to avoid the crowds a park would bring, Most did not want Castle Peak to be mined. The much larger molybdenum deposit on Thompson Creek near Challis had not yet been discovered.

We went back up 4th of July Creek and looked for the lake. The creek in the meadow that had stopped us before was only a trickle and there were ruts that showed the road crossed it now. We found cars parked by a tumbledown cabin. Even a Volkswagen Beetle was there. A signed trail led off to the right from the parking area. The year before we had stopped too soon and followed a jeep road part way to Phyllis Lake. At 4th of July Lake, we encountered a convention of mosquitoes, but the lake was in a meadow of shooting stars and buttercups with orange-gray cliffs of Patterson Peak above it. I sat there enjoying that mountain wall and the wildflowers. Leslie and Neal fished and Hilary and Stuart played at fishing with willow poles and bits of line baited with flowers.

After that first day I made the hiking more fun for the older kids and myself by getting a babysitter for Hilary and Stuart. Winnie at the cafe at Obsidian had suggested I call Peggy Bitton who had a daughter the right age.

Sally, age 11, babysat at her house with the help of her mother. Sally wore a walking cast because she had fallen out of a tree at the beginning of the summer and broken her leg. Her father, Max, had started an outfitting business, Mystic Saddle Ranch, in the Sawtooths that summer. I hoped that because we knew the Bittons, maybe Wayne would be open to the idea of going on a pack trip the next summer,

The first time I had Sally babysit, Leslie, Neal, and I hiked to Marshall Lake in the Sawtooths. We went the old way from the road up Meadow Creek near the airport at Stanley. That road had not yet been closed by private property so the distance was only three miles. After Doug arrived from scout camp, we also hiked to the Upper Bench Lakes and Sawtooth Lake.

The Bench Lakes are five lakes in a string below the pleated wall of Mt. Heyburn, and I had already been to the first two with Wayne and Doug 13 years before. Only the first two lakes are on the trail, but I decided to try to go to some of the upper lakes because we found a path leading in that direction. At the third Bench lake, we met a chunky young woman with wild frizzy hair, who had a string of fish. When Doug asked her how she had caught so many, she said with a wicked grin, "Cannibalism. Those brook trout like to eat each other. Here's a fish. Cut it up and use it for bait and I guarantee you'll catch fish." She then gave us directions for reaching the fourth lake where she said the fishing was superb. We had to climb over boulders and up a slippery scree slope, but we reached the lake. With a chunk of brook trout, Leslie caught her first fish there. She was both pleased and horrified, "They really do eat their brothers and sisters!"

The week after Sally babysat, my parents visited us at the cabin for the first time since we had built it. Having them come visit at the cabin was my idea and it would give me an excuse to spend more time there. They would want to hike and their presence would encourage the children's hiking. Because the cabin was still so primitive they stayed at a motel called Swiss Villa across the highway from what had been Trigger Jim's. By then a subdivision, power lines and an airstrip were going up next to Swiss Villa. I didn't see any 12-story turquoise hotel going up like Harrah's at South Tahoe. Still I was afraid it wouldn't be long before one was built. Jim Decker had sold his business at Obsidian, keeping only his house and the post office. They had moved the post office from beside the cafe to next to their house.

When my parents arrived, they looked older than I remembered because I still thought of them as looking as they had when we left California 13 years earlier. My mother's hair was more than half white, and her solid figure had sagged. My father was mostly bald, and he had developed a little potbelly. When I asked my mother what she thought of the cabin, she looked around, chewed on her lip, and said, "You've started quite a project here."

Maybe she really thought we were crazy. I was disappointed because I wanted her to be enthusiastic. I wanted my parents to see my family as a hiking family like my brother's and sister's, I wanted my parents to think we were carrying on the family tradition. I had the idea that if they did, they would also think I was a good mother.

When I asked my parents what hikes they'd like to do, my father said, "I'd like to go to Sawtooth Lake. The pictures I've seen of it are beautiful."

I was reluctant because I had just taken Doug, Leslie, and Neal there the week before and knew it was too far for Hilary and Stuart. I suggested Fourth of July Lake, but when my father learned about the bad road, he refused to go there. When I said I'd stay with Hilary and Stuart or get a babysitter for them, my mother said, "Well, then we won't go."

Wayne was back at work in Caldwell but all the rest of us hiked to Sawtooth Lake. The trailhead is about five miles north of Stanley and five miles up a dirt road called Iron Creek. As the kids and my parents started out they formed a funny-looking procession. Doug wore a white sailor cap Tom had brought back from the Navy and carried a backpack with our lunches and the emergency ponchos. Behind him my father wore the red beret my mother had given him so she could keep track of him while he took pictures. He lugged his camera equipment in a brown leather bag slung over one shoulder. The bag weighed at least 25 pounds, and I worried that he'd have a heart attack trying to carry it so far. Neal hurried along, his freckled face rosy from trying to keep up with Doug and his grandpa. Now and then he glanced back to check that Hilary and Stuart were still there. He always kept close track of them perhaps because he once got lost from us in Winnemucca, Nevada, when he was four and had never forgotten how scared he had been.

Leslie wore a small blue knapsack and the gold rims of her glasses matched the sun streaks in her hair. Hilary's little pack was red and she chewed on the ends of her long ash-blonde hair as she walked. Stuart, skinny and tall for three, wore another of the white sailor hats over his blonde curls. He had lost the last piece of his blanket but he still put two fingers in his mouth now and then. My mother wore a green calico sunbonnet, cats-eye-shaped sunglasses, and a windbreaker tied around her waist. I wore jeans, a paisley print shirt, and the pale blue sunbonnet I had made when I was 16.

The first part of the trail led up and down through a lodgepole forest. After a couple of miles, we came to a junction. One arm of the sign said Sawtooth Lake 3.6. Stuart stopped and sat down. "Come on, Stuart, we'll never get to the lake if we don't keep going," said Leslie.

"I need lifesavers," he said. I gave him one. Then Doug took him by the hand. He said, "Come walk with me. We'll be trucks, what kind do you want to be?"

"Coca cola."

"Here is your gas gauge," said Doug, hanging his compass around Stuart's neck. "When I look at it and it says it's empty, I'll give you some gas. Now, go." he said, giving Stuart a gentle push. "Remember you are a truck and make a noise like one." "Rrr," Stuart said as he started up the trail.

After three long switchbacks, a creek crossing, and several short switchbacks we reached the ledges above Alpine Lake. There we ate lunch and looked down on the lake's blue-green water that shaded to mint green in the shallows. Above it rose the cracked cliffs of Alpine Peak. It began to rain as we started on again, but a big patch of blue sky appeared just as we decided to turn back, so we kept going. To my surprise all of us reached Sawtooth Lake. I carried Hilary for the last mile but Stuart walked all the way, still pretending to be a truck. When we reached the view of the immense bluish-silver platter of Sawtooth Lake and the granite slabs of Mt Regan, my father insisted we pose in front of it for pictures. But my mother lay down and refused to sit up for his photos.

As we neared the trailhead on the way back, Stuart leaned over, examined the trail, and said, "Gremlins stretched the trail. It's longer than this morning. Pointing at a low outcrop that ran across the trail, he said, "See those cracks? That's where they stretched it."

"Come on Stuart, don't be silly. Hurry up, the Sawtooth Hotel will be closed before we get there," said Neal, pulling Stuart by the arm. My father had told the kids he would take them out for dinner when we got back.

"Stop it, ow!" said Stuart, who tripped and fell. I picked him up and carried him the rest of the way. After the hike, I felt I had proved my kids were good hikers and was proud of them. My three-year-old had walked almost eight miles!

As we ate hamburgers at the hotel, my father said, "Sawtooth Lake and the rest of the Sawtooths are so beautiful they should be a national park."

"I don't want that. We couldn't keep our cabin."

"That's not true. Owners can keep cabins in national parks at least for their whole life."

"That's not long enough. What about the kids? Also, there would be way too many people."

After my parents left, Neal begged me to take him up a mountain. His brown eyes intense, he said, "Grandpa asked me if I had climbed any mountains lately, and I had to say no. Aren't there any mountains we could climb here?"

When Neal was four my parents had taken him up a little mountain called Tahoe Mountain, at Fallen Leaf. It had a two-mile trail to the top. Most of the peaks in the Sawtooths required ropes, but on the map there was a trail to a lookout on top of Horton Peak. It was in the White Clouds just across the valley from the cabin. Near sundown each day we could see the little cube of the lookout shining white. Horton Peak was a high sagebrush hill, with timber only on the north side of its main ridge.

Stuart had just thrown up a couple of times, so I didn't think he could make it up the peak if we went up the next day. We had only one more day before I had to take the kids home so they could register for school. Even though Leslie was only 11, I asked her to take care of Hilary and Stuart the next day. I took Doug with me to encourage Neal and carry our lunches. I worried a little about leaving Leslie with Hilary and Stuart. We had no telephone, so in an emergency she would have to run 1/4 mile to the Hunts, who had the nearest cabin with a phone, but she was old enough to do that. I thought I could see our cabin well enough from the mountain to see if anything was going wrong.

Next morning, as we started up the trail through sagebrush and dry grass, stickers worked their way into my socks. All three of us wore the high-topped black sneakers we called basketball shoes.

After climbing a few switchbacks, I stopped and pointed out the cabin to Neal. He took off his dark glasses to see better and said, "It looks like a little square bug."

It was much farther away than I had expected, but it was too late to take Doug back to babysit. Soon the trail disappeared in sagebrush. After that we continued up a long, long sagebrush slope, dodging ground squirrel holes. Neal said, "Ow, the stickers are killing me."

We stopped, and I tried to pull the stickers out of his socks, but there were hundreds. We'd never reach the top if he had to wear those socks, and I wanted him to feel successful in climbing this mountain. I said, "Just put your shoes back on with no socks. They'll be all right this last little bit, and on the way down it won't matter.

At last we reached the old white lookout and found it unoccupied and several of its window panes broken. From it, Castle Peak, the highest of the White Clouds, looked as though it had been fired in a kiln into smooth white porcelain on the side towards us. Neal said, "I want to go right up to those white mountains. What do you think they're made of?"

The whole hike, counting the drive to and from the trailhead, took only four hours but all the way back I worried about leaving Leslie with Hilary and Stuart so long. Back at the cabin, the potty chair was sitting in the driveway. When I opened the door, Leslie motioned us away and said, "Ssh, they're napping. Stuart has diarrhea now. I hope it was all right to put the potty chair outside. It smelled so awful I couldn't stand it."

I smiled and said it was fine, but later I wondered how she would have handled a real emergency.

The next morning, Doug said, "We need a place for Neal to carve his mountain. We need a boat log like the one at Fallen Leaf."

"There aren't any good logs near the cabin," I said, "The big one has too much bark and Dad's cutting up the other for firewood."

Doug rummaged around, found a paper plate, and on it listed all the hikes we had taken from the cabin so far with the initials of those who had gone on the hike. Then he said, "Here, Neal. You write Horton Peak here and N, M, and D and whatever else you want."

Neal wrote "Stickers" and Doug added, "See Castle Peak."

Doug taped the plate to the refrigerator. Until he went off to work at the scout camp for the summer a couple of years later, he kept a hike record on paper plates. I wish now I had saved those plates.

Back at home the kids and I started helping Wayne and the candidates for various offices put flyers and door knockers on peoples porches. We especially took around flyers for Cecil Andrus for governor. Wayne and I kept going to various campaign events and let some out-of-town workers use our phone. Workers and candidates often dropped in just to talk to Wayne or to me if he wasn't there.

For trick or treating on Halloween Neal, then eight, dressed up as a politician in a little suit that used to belong to Doug. He pinned signs on his chest and back "Vote for me. I'll save the White Clouds."

We were all relieved when Andrus won and managed to stop the mine on Castle Peak. Wayne was doubly relieved because Bill did not win his race for Congress and came back to work at the office.

Stuart's first hike. Frog Lake near the Carson Pass in California.

Leslie on Baron Divide.

CHAPTER 8: THE OLD PACK TRIP

Now that I am 85 and find it difficult to hike more than a couple of miles I look back on the hikes Wayne and I did with the kids with longing. Even the kids like to remember the trip they call our old pack trip. It was the first multi-day backcountry trip we did as a family.

In the spring of 1971, I asked Wayne if we could talk to Max Bitton about a pack trip. The babysitter Sally whom I had used the summer before was his daughter. I was surprised and very pleased when Wayne said "yes, we could talk to him." If we planned it right it would allow me to see the heart of the Sawtooths. We would get to see some of the places people like our former neighbors the Banks had talked about, places like Toxaway and Cramer Lakes.

Wayne arranged with the Bittons for three riding horses so our younger kids wouldn't have to walk all the time. From Frostline kits I sewed down sleeping bags for the three older children. Stuffing the bags spread down all over the house but I thought that was worth it. I had sewed sleeping bags for Wayne and myself the year before for the raft trip and had found that sewing each one took several days.

In June we took all the kids to the cabin so Wayne could attend the state bar convention in Sun Valley. I drove down for a luncheon and a couple of dinners. While Wayne was at the convention, his oldest sister Marjorie called to tell him his mother had died. She was only 71 but had a heart condition. It was very sad. His mother had given me produce and fabric so I could can and sew. The Christmas when Stuart was six months old, she had paid for a plane ticket for me to take Hilary and Stuart to see my parents when my sister Dodie was visiting with her first child, Jimmy. She took me to the luncheon in Nampa in 1964 where she was named runner up in the Idaho Mother of the Year contest. When Hilary was born and she heard that Neal had stuck nails all over a block of cheese, she had sent him a big tricycle on the Greyhound bus. In the card with it she said, "Here is something to take Neal's mind off the new baby."

We spent two days going to Buhl for the funeral. Getting ready for it required shopping because the kids had not taken any good clothes to the cabin. After the funeral, we left Doug in Buhl to work for his uncles, Wesley and Bruce. They ran the lumberyard Wayne's dad had started in 1945 and invited Doug to help them for the next few weeks.

When we returned to the cabin, an electrician client of Wayne's, Del Rice, spent two days installing the circuit breaker box and showing us how to put in junction boxes, outlets and fixtures ourselves. It was amazing we were going to have electricity at last. I wouldn't have to plug things in with extension cords to the power pole any longer. I looked forward to cooking on our old stove instead of in the electric fry pan, I would no longer have to heat water in the turkey roaster, and we could have more than one light on at night. We could even get an electric heater. It was a very cold June so we all had to wear lots of sweaters and wool shirts while we did the wiring.

Wayne put in the junction boxes and wired the simple, porcelain light fixtures. Each fixture was just a place to screw in one light bulb. Both of us learned to install outlets. Mr. Rice said, "First, you strip the insulation off the ends of the wires with the knife like this. Next you wind the bare ends of the black and the white wires around the brass screws in the outlet, and tighten the screws. Then you attach the bare end of the green wire to the outlet box to ground it."

At first the wires came unwound when I screwed in the brass screws, but soon I got the hang of it. It took several days to finish. The four younger kids were too young to help.

The inside walls of the cabin were still bare two-by-fours except for a wall of leftover siding we had put up between the two downstairs bedrooms. In late July Wayne hired the carpenter, J.G. Nicholson, who had helped him build the cabin, to build us a front porch and stairs to the loft. After he did this, the cabin seemed much more livable.

To get ready for our pack trip the second week of August, we had practiced riding horses at the Bitton's ranch at Middleton near Caldwell. I took the kids up to the cabin a week or so before the trip to get them used to the altitude and to hiking. My mother came to visit us there while my dad went on a Sierra Club trip in California. She flew to Hailey in a plane that was so small it looked more like a Volkswagen bus than an airplane. I didn't see how she had the courage to go up in such a rickety plane, but then she told me about flying to New York to visit her mother with me when I was six months old. It took three days, because planes didn't fly at night then, and she and I spent the nights in tourist courts (now called motels). For her visit to us in the Sawtooths, she again stayed at Swiss Villa. While she was there we hiked up the jeep road from the 4th of July Creek trailhead that we had been lost on two years before. From the end of the road we followed a path to pretty Phyllis Lake. When some motorcyclists passed us on the way up my mother yelled "Lazy!" at them. Of course, they couldn't hear her over their engines, but at least she told them what she thought.

Doug went to scout camp at Warm Lake near Cascade the week before the pack trip, and Wayne drove over to get him. On the way back they stopped at Stanley for Doug to do his laundry. He insisted on drying it in the dryer instead of hanging it to dry back at the cabin. When a woman put her wet laundry in a dryer that had just stopped, one they had planned to use, neither of them noticed it had stopped. Wayne was very annoyed. He didn't want to wait through that load to dry Doug's clothes. When Doug refused to take his wet laundry back to the cabin and hang it up to dry, Wayne went off and left him there. When Wayne got to the cabin he said, "I've been practicing law for 14 years and I never get to take the vacation I want to and always have kids on the vacation. I shouldn't have to wait two hours for a kid who can't pay attention."

He lay down on the bed and shut his eyes.

So I got in the car and drove to Stanley to look for Doug. I found him south of town walking up the highway with his laundry bag over his shoulder. With that beginning to the pack trip, I hoped it would go a lot better than Wayne's drive back from the scout camp had done.

The next morning we met the Bittons at their ranch near Obsidian and then started the trip from the Pettit Lake trailhead, two miles north of our cabin. Wayne, Doug and Leslie hiked ahead, taking the first turn to walk. Max, wiry, gray-haired, and as weather beaten as old canvas, led the pack string from his chestnut horse, Mac. There were also three heavy-boned packhorses Moose, Cocoa, and Dandy.

Behind them, Neal rode a bay horse called Little Lady. His freckles were shaded by one of the white sailor hats my brother Tom had brought back from the Navy. Neal had decorated this one with colored markers. I followed on a larger bay, Big Lady, with Stuart sitting behind me, his arms clasped around my waist. I also had to lead an Appaloosa, Pepper, which six-year-old Hilary rode. As we started out, at first I felt so happy to be on a pack trip that riding felt like floating on air. Ahead I caught glimpses of the cliffs that lined the canyon of Pettit Lake's inlet where the trail went and looked forward to getting closer to them.

As soon as we started up the canyon Big Lady slowed down and Pepper got her feet tangled in the lead rope. When I got off to untangle the rope, Stuart fell off in the bushes. Luckily he wasn't hurt. The other walkers and riders and the pack string were all far ahead before I got the lead straightened, put Stuart back on the horse, and remounted myself. This was not working out well. I was all by myself and was afraid of the horses getting tangled up again. Leading Pepper was much more difficult than I had thought. Then I found that the trail kept crossing the creek between Pettit and Alice lakes, and it was 15 or 20 feet wide and rushing. At each ford the horses plunged down the bank into the water and then bounded up the far side, making me bounce in the saddle.

We stopped to eat lunch at the second ford. After lunch, Hilary, Wayne and I walked behind the pack string while Leslie, Neal, and Doug took their turns on the horses. I was glad I didn't have to ride any more for awhile. On the bay horse Little Lady, Doug rode in a cowboy shirt and wire-rimmed glasses, with Stuart perched behind him, his arms tight around Doug's waist

By mid-afternoon, we had reached Alice Lake and started along it. Across the lake rose a mountain called El Capitan. It looked like a skyscraper that was the shape of a flame blown to a slant. Granite peninsulas with whitebark pines and the narrow crowns of subalpine firs enclosed the lake. Unnamed dragon mountains barred the head of the lake. Behind them clouds had built up and it started to sprinkle. Suddenly, just ahead of me, Little Lady's feet clattered on the rocks and she lurched. Stuart let go and fell off. "Stuie," Hilary screamed. Little Lady began to trot. Doug fell off and the horse dragged him along by the foot. "Oh no," I gasped, dashing forward.

On the grass on the opposite side of the trail, Stuart sat up, so I knew he was all right. By the time I reached Doug, Max had caught Little Lady, and freed Doug's foot. Doug was covered with dust and had torn his shirt, and skinned his elbow and cheek. We were lucky he was only skinned! Wayne poured water from his canteen onto a bandanna and washed Doug s cheek. "Have you seen my glasses?" Doug said, squirming under Wayne s hand. Hilary searched in the willows at the edge of the lake and found his glasses on a branch. Max said, "Doug, you OK?" Doug nodded.

"Get right back on so you won't be spooked."

I hadn't thought riding the horses would be so dangerous, but after this I worried most of the time. I had wanted so much to go on a pack trip, but it was turning out to be way too dangerous. Then as we started on again, lightning flashed, followed by thunder, and a downpour. We soon reached campsites beside Alice Lake, but Max said we couldn't camp there because there was no grass for the horses. We had to go another mile to Twin Lakes. First, we stopped and put on our nylon rain ponchos. Stuart and Hilary's were so long Wayne had to trim them with his Swiss knife. After a short climb over rocks we came to Twin Lakes, which were right under the dragon mountains.

When the kids and I set up our umbrella tent, we found we couldn't fit all seven sleeping bags into it. We hadn't used it for six or seven years so I had forgotten how small it was. And the last time we used it we had fewer kids and the ones we had were much smaller. We managed to fit five bags in with Stuart's across the heads of the others. Max loaned Wayne and Doug some canvas horse mantis to make themselves a tent. As soon as we had the tents set up it stopped raining, luckily, because our agreement with Max was we would provide the food and I was cooking. One of the dishes I remember making on this trip was canned chow mein with canned chicken on canned crunchy Chinese noodles.

In the evening the older kids fished and Stuart built rock dams on a tiny stream. While sitting beside the shore's shooting stars, I looked up flowers in the book I had bought on Rocky Mountain wildflowers. There were many I had never seen in California. I didn't get much chance to look them up because Hilary kept tangling her fishing line and wanting me to untangle it.

The next morning Max told us Snowyside Pass was going to be difficult because of the snow. He asked for volunteers to ride. Leslie volunteered because she had just taken riding lessons at Camp Tamanawis, a girl scout camp in eastern Idaho. Doug also volunteered - to get over being afraid. I was glad not to have to ride,

Wayne, Neal, Stuart, and I hiked up under the gray cliffs of Snowyside Peak to the pass. On the far side the trail led across snow for 200 yards. We stamped a path across it for the horses. Below the snowbank, the trail zigzagged down to two turquoise ponds in the rocks. At the first one we stopped for lunch and to wait for the horses. The grassy places around it were covered with the white curls of parrot's beak. It was one of the flowers in my new book.

After lunch, Wayne rode, leading Pepper with Hilary and I rode with Stuart. The trail led down to the big blue expanse of Toxaway Lake. Half way along that big lake, we took a side trail over Sand Mountain Pass. In the middle of a long switchback, Little Lady flipped up her back hooves and sent Wayne flying down into small firs and juniper bushes. When I started to dismount to help Wayne, Max slid off his horse and said, "It's not safe to get off here. I'll deal with it."

Max tied up his horse and the pack string to trees, slithered down, caught Little Lady and led her back to the trail. Doug retrieved Wayne's cowboy hat from farther down the hillside. Wayne dusted pine needles and twigs off his jeans and work shirt, and scrambled back to the trail. He asked if Little Lady was all right. Max suppressed a laugh, shook his head and said, "She's okay. You didn't by any chance get the lead rope under her tail, did ya?"

Of course, that was what had happened. Wayne suggested to me that we just turn around and go back to Toxaway for the rest of the week. I was scared of riding, but it would be too disappointing not to see all the country we had planned to see. Besides it would be a failure and we'd never take another pack trip. That would be terrible. I shook my head and kept on walking.

That evening tree shadows cast long spires across the blue water of Edna Lake. At sunset the silvery peaks and ridges above it turned to a city of gold. Just then a teen-aged boy in a black cowboy hat rode up. It was Max's son Jeff, 16, come to help his dad. He said, "The Wheelers canceled, and Mom thought you could use some help. Here's some hamburger and Russian tea."

The Russian tea was delicious. I think it was probably instant tea mixed with Tang and spices. What a relief! With Jeff to lead Pepper and to help with the horses, we could continue the trip with much less danger. (When Jeff grew up he carried on his father's outfitting business and ran the stables at Redfish for many years.)

Jeff's presence was vital the following day when three of the horses tried to run down the trail toward Grandjean during lunch at Hidden Lake. Max and Jeff had to run after them. After lunch we climbed Cramer Divide. Doug, Hilary, Stuart, and I rode, and Jeff led Pepper with Hilary. At the summit we looked down on unbroken snow ahead.

Max told us to get off and lead the horses over the snow while he and Jeff brought their own horses and the pack string down. There were many switchbacks and they were all invisible under the snow. It was hard for Hilary and me to keep hold of our horses while we crossed the snowbanks, especially Pepper, since Hilary was still afraid of her. We didn't find out until after the trip that this was the first time Max and Jeff had gone over Cramer Divide.

That night we camped at Upper Cramer Lake below a 1500-foot wall of cliffs. In one low point an orange tower stuck up like the tip of an arrow, a formation called The Arrowhead. Hilary recognized it as the House Rock she had seen from the other side at Hell Roaring Lake. She had said it was her House Rock because she was the first one to notice it. After that it was always a special landmark for us. However, it is no longer there because the March 2020 earthquake north of the Sawtooths knocked it down.

The next day, we descended three and a half miles to the bottom of Redfish Canyon at Flatrock Junction, where one trail goes down the canyon to Redfish Lake and the other, climbs to Alpine Lake. I was one of those riding, and Wayne walked. When I dismounted at Alpine Lake my feet were numb. When Wayne, Doug and Neal reached the lake an hour after the rest of us, Wayne said, "If I'd known it was straight up to get here we'd have skipped Alpine Lake."

After dinner, as Wayne had promised, he watched Hilary and Stuart, while Leslie and I hiked 2 miles to Baron Divide. She and I reached the divide at sunset. Back across Redfish Canyon, the wall above Cramer Lakes glowed as though candles burned within it. The pinkish-orange light tinted Leslie's face red. Beyond the divide we looked down on Upper Baron and Baron lakes, dark blue ovals set below a wall of immense granite folds that look like a row of rockets. Leslie turned to me, green eyes shining, and said, "Thanks, Mom, for bringing me here." For me that was the best moment of the trip.

Max, Jeff, Doug, and Neal fished the next day. When Max showed no signs of getting ready to leave by lunch time, Wayne, Leslie, Hilary, Stuart, and I started down the trail. This was supposed to be our last day. We knew it was five and a half miles to the boat landing and we didn't know if there would be a boat there to get us or not. By trail it was still five more miles from the landing to the lodge. It was a long hike just to the boat landing with tired kids. We had to carry Stuart some of the way. When we reached the junction with the trail down to the boat dock, I took the kids to the beach to wade. After an hour I left them with Leslie while I went back up to where Wayne was still waiting. Finally at 5:15 Max, the horses, and the boys arrived. Max turned his horse to go down to the dock. Wayne put out his hand and said, "You can't take the horses on the boat."

"Boat, what boat? Our horse trailers are in the parking lot down there."

"The parking lot isn't down there. It is at the other end of the lake by the lodge, five more miles."

Max snorted and wheeled his horse around to head up the other trail. We would find out later that he had never been down Redfish canyon to the lake before. Wayne and I went down to the landing to wait for a boat. In about ten minutes a boat from the lodge came to pick up some kayakers and we rode back with them. We reached the lodge in time to call the ranch and have the horse trailers brought to Redfish by the time Max and the boys got there.

On the way back to the cabin we went to the hot baths. The hot water in the hot springs felt more wonderful than it ever had before.

I had reached one of my lifetime goals of a pack trip with my children, and my heart was smiling. But next time I decided we would walk, not ride and just have horses carry our food and gear. Two days after the trip, I didn't want to go back to Caldwell when Wayne went back to work. I told him I wanted to stay at the cabin with the kids for another week. He wasn't happy about this, but he said it would be all right if I did.

The five kids below Saddleback Lakes

CHAPTER 9:
SECRET TRAILS

During that week after the pack trip I wanted to go to some of the secret places our former neighbors the Banks had gone to with scouts and their church group. The place I most wanted to go they called Shangri-La and they said it was like Yosemite with a very high rock wall above three lakes. Most people called the rock wall the Elephants Perch. I am not sure if I got directions from them or just figured out how to reach Shangri-La from the then-new topographic maps available for part of the Sawtooths and White Clouds.

We had finished our pack trip on Friday. On Sunday as soon as Wayne left the cabin for home I got the kids ready to go try to find Shangri-La Lakes. I took food for dinner as well as lunch to make sure the kids would have enough energy to get there if we could find the way. The shuttle boat on Redfish Lake held 12 and took about 15 minutes to go to the upper end, where the trail up Redfish Canyon started. The boat got us there about 10:30 A.M.

From the dock the children scampered out and started up the trail. I can't remember now who led, but Doug was especially eager to see Shangri la.

The kids refused to wear hats, but I wore my usual sunbonnet. I had boots but the kids just wore sneakers. This was before running shoes were common.

The ranger, Ralph Cisco, had told me that the route to the lakes started at a logjam on Redfish Creek beside a big campsite about two miles up the trail.

Once across the log jam we had to fight our way through alder bushes to see where we were going. Just above them was a little pile of rocks. Pointing, Stuart said, "Look, there's one of Grandpa's ducks!"

"Silly, Grandpa's in California. It's just a pile of rocks." Hilary scowled at him through her bangs.

"It probably shows us which way to go," said Neal. "Look, there s another one up there."

Doug led off up the granite slabs with the rest of us trailing behind.

Stuart walked just ahead of me at the end of the procession. He and I gradually got farther behind. "How much farther is it?" Stuart whined.

Ahead the kids had stopped to talk to two other hikers. When Stuart and I came up to them, Doug asked them, "How long did it take you to get to the lakes."

"Two and a half hours. You better not try to take your little ones up there. They ll never make it."

"Yes, they will," said Doug, "You don't know these kids."

"Come," he said, taking Stuart by the hand. "You can find the ducks for us, show us the right way to go."

That worked magic on Stuart. He literally ran to the next little pile of rocks, waited for us to reach it and then scampered ahead.

Beyond the rock slabs the cairns led us to a path that ran below a 30-foot rock wall for several hundred yards. Beyond the wall the path went up toward and then along below the orange wall of the Elephant's Perch. There it was, a secret trail. From what the Banks had said about Shangri La, I had a feeling there was a secret trail, and now we had found it.

Below the Elephant's Perch the path led up a steep gravelly slope where I had to give Hilary a hand. Stuart was still scampering up from rock pile to rock pile. When he skidded he just put a hand down to keep from sliding back and got right up again.

Then the path dropped down to the creek and crossed it. Leslie looked at her watch and said, "It's lunch time. Can we have lunch now?"

"I'm hungry," said Stuart.

So we sat on boulders beside the creek and ate our sandwiches. pieces of apple, Windmill cookies, and M&Ms.

After lunch it was only another couple hundred yards to a narrow pond right under the Elephant's Perch. It was the first of the three lakes. It took only five minutes to follow the path to a second, much bigger lake. I looked at my watch. It had taken us only two hours to reach the lakes from the main trail. My four and six year old were faster than the men we had talked to.

After the kids went down to the shore and looked around Doug and Leslie started fishing from a big granite outcrop that slanted down to the water. Hilary and Stuart began making a village for the matchbox cars Stuart had hidden in his pack. Neal kept following the path around the lake from granite outcrop to marshy bay and then another outcrop.

I went after Neal to get him to stay put. As I did I heard yelling from Leslie and Doug, but thought they could probably solve their own problem. When I caught up with Neal and told him to stop he asked, "Can I go to the next lake? The map shows one more. Look!" He grabbed the map I had in my hand and pointed.

I told him that I would go with him as soon as I told the other kids and found out if any of them wanted to come. When I got back to the big slanting outcrop, Doug was there fishing but Leslie had disappeared. "She got her lure in my hair, and I told her to go away."

He pointed to the other side of the lake, showing me where she was. The little kids were playing happily with their little village. I then took Neal to the upper lake, but it was not as pretty because the big orange wall was far away. When we got back to the granite slab where I had left the other kids, Doug was helping Stuart fish with his pole, Hilary was playing with Stuart's two little cars in the village.

By then it was 5 o'clock. I had arranged for the boat to come back for us at 8:30. So I built a fire, cooked macaroni dinner and stirred up some instant pudding. When it was ready I went down to the shore and called to Leslie. Finally, she noticed me pointing in the direction of Redfish and came back across the creek with a big grin and a string of eight fish. When Doug saw the fish he scowled and turned away. He had caught only one.

After dinner, we started down the path to the main trail. In spite of having eaten dinner the kids were slow. They straggled down to the log jam and down the main trail toward the inlet. By the time we neared the turnoff for the half mile walk to the boat landing, it was 8:15. Afraid of being stranded with no equipment overnight I sent Doug running ahead to be sure we didn't miss the boat. Then I picked up Stuart and carried him a few yards. Hilary, who had whined on the way up, seemed to go much faster on the way down, almost as if she could smell the ice cream at the lodge. The boat was late because it had engine trouble, which worked out well for us.

I felt very pleased that we had successfully reached our destination, but I soon found out that Shangri La was its unofficial name, The Forest Service used its official name, Saddleback Lakes and the Elephant's Perch was the Saddleback. The name Shangri La had made it seem secret, like the mythical place in James Hilton's novel, *Lost Horizon*, where people lived nearly forever.

Later that same week in 1971 I decided to try to take the kids to another place that might be hard to find and maybe had a secret trail. I got the idea from a topographic map of part of the White Clouds, the mountains which were across Sawtooth Valley from our cabin. We had seen a sign on the trail to 4th of July Lake that said Born Lakes 2 3/4. The sign encouraged me to try to find Born Lakes. We had found that lake by following the wheel ruts across the creek in the meadow and up past a modern cabin to a parking area beside a tumbledown log cabin. A sign for 4th of July Lake pointed to the right across the main creek. Farther up the road stood three buildings that looked like railroad cars covered with silver paper. Later I learned they were the home of a miner named Elmer Enderlin who had developed several mines and built some of the roads in the 4th of July Creek area.

The topographic map showed a trail going north over a 10,000-foot divide from the Born Lakes sign. On the other side of it a trail down Warm Springs Creek led all the way to the Salmon River. A cluster of the tiny lakes labeled Born Lakes was at the head of that creek but the map didn't show any trail to them. Later in the week after the pack trip I set out with the kids to find Born Lakes.

Driving up the 4th of July Road was just as rocky and scary as before, but the mud had solidified and the puddles and tiny creeks had dried up. So the kids and I reached the trailhead without worrying about getting stuck. I worried only about flat tires. Above us all around loomed gray peaks topped with cliffs and gullies. Just imagine me in my sunbonnet trailed by five kids in sneakers, scraggly hats, and dirt-streaked shirts. Doug carried our lunches and two ponchos to make a shelter in case of rain. To start out on the trail we first had to wade 4th of July Creek. That was not as hard as wading it in June 1969 because the water was much lower. We struggled up the rocky trail under lodgepole pines, through marshy meadows and across three more creeks to the sign, Born Lakes 2 3/4. From it we climbed a steep trail to a pond in the rocks and then to the 10,000-foot divide.

"Are we there yet? How far up are these lakes, anyway?" Stuart and Hilary complained. Years later a historian researching mining claims in the White Clouds discovered the name of the miner for whom the lakes are named was really Boorn, not Born.

I took Stuart by the hand. "Let's play 20 questions." The game took us up to the summit of the divide. On top, Hilary looked across the valley and pointed, "Look, Neal, your white mountains!"

"Wow, there they are!"

Across the canyon rose the slanted wall of creamy white rock and gravel, decorated at the base with dark green trees. We took the trail down to a flat green meadow, labeled on the map as Ants Basin. I would find out later it wasn't named for ants but for a miner named Antz.

In its grass a sandy trail led off to the left and disappeared over the edge of the basin. A faint path led to the right toward the lakes and ended in the grass.

We went to the right and from where the path ended we walked downhill along a stream at the edge of a big bed of talus. Then we walked up the canyon along the lower edge of the talus. Soon we came to two small lakes in grass and lodgepoles in a basin surrounded by pale orange mountains with cliffs at their tops. Here Doug and Leslie and Neal began to fish while I got out the lunch. After lunch Neal came with me to see if the third and largest lake had more or bigger fish. We could see several big fish in it, so I left Neal there and went back to the first lakes to get the other kids.

We spent at least an hour at this upper lake with the three older kids fishing. Nobody caught a fish until Neal threw some salmon eggs into the water. I told him this was illegal but the fish started biting. Still, they didn't stick onto the lures. Then Doug went and caught a grasshopper. That seemed to make one fish open its mouth wider and he caught one about ten inches long. Seeing this Hilary and Stuart ran around catching grasshoppers. By the time we left Doug, Leslie and Neal had each caught a big fish and some smaller ones. I think the largest was 16 inches. I had brought food for supper but had left it in the car, so about 5 o'clock I insisted we start back in spite of the fish bonanza. None of us have ever caught such big or so many fish in Born Lakes since.

Five o'clock wasn't really soon enough because when we reached the steep slope above Ants Basin Stuart sat down and said, "My feet hurt. Do we have to climb back up?"

"Yes. we didn't bring our sleeping bags." I gave him a few M&Ms and he straggled up to the corner of the first switchback. "I can't go any farther," he said, sitting down again. So I picked him up and carried him to the top of the divide. This was hard to do because by then he weighed 45 pounds.

On the drive back to the cabin I stopped at a campsite that lay below the worst part of the road, built a fire and cooked supper for the kids. That made them all stop whining.

Because there was no path to Born Lakes except for a few feet in Ants Basin, I felt this was our secret trail and no one else's. My neighbors said their church group had never been into the White Clouds, let alone to Born Lakes

Now of course the route along the side and base of the talus is a well-worn path. The main trail comes up Warm Springs Canyon to the first three lakes, not to Antz Basin. Also the lakes, the basin, and most of the White Clouds are within the Cecil D. Andrus White Clouds Wilderness.

Petrolyphs at Wees Bar in the Snake River canyon.

CHAPTER 10: A BACK OPERATION

In October of 1971, we hauled a Franklin stove from Montgomery Ward, a kitchen sink in a steel cabinet, and a set of shutters to the cabin in our Ford pickup. Along our way, aspens brightened the dark green pines and firs with gold and orange. I had made the shutters myself, using the circular saw Wayne's father had given us from his lumberyard years before. Fitting the shutters to the windows was difficult because they were wooden Anderson windows and they opened with metal arms. I had to cut insets in the outer corners of each shutter to fit around these arms and I had painted the shutters bright green to cheer up the brown of the cabin. Wayne, Doug, Leslie, and I had carried in the sink cabinet and Franklin stove. It took all four of us to lift each of these things. The stove weighed at least 300 pounds, so my share was about 75 pounds.

I don't remember my back hurting after I had helped carry in the sink and stove. However, one day the following April when I reached over into the back seat of the car to get a box of tissue, my back started to hurt. Just before that Wayne had me help lift the TV down from its high shelf to go to the repair shop, and a couple of days later when the car wouldn't start, had asked me to push the car while he tried to start it. I didn't realize I could have said no. I didn't say no because he was already cross with me because he said the day before I had gone to the back side of Bogus Basin without telling him. I think he was watching the TV in the Pioneer Lodge at the time and didn't even notice I was talking.

Two days after I reached for the tissue my right leg felt as though it had pins sticking into it. When I went to the doctor, he said it was arthritis and gave me some exercises to do. One of my father's friends had arthritis and could no longer hike because of it, so the diagnosis filled me with dread. I had been looking forward to doing more hikes from our cabin and to going on a family trip to Banff and Jasper.

My back might have recovered if I hadn't gone on an expedition with my cub scout den a few weeks later. My co-leader, Margaret Langan, and I decided to take the cubs on a hike to the Wees Bar petroglyphs near Swan Falls in the Snake River Canyon near Kuna. Petroglyphs are designs scratched into rock by ancient peoples. Idahoans like to keep places like this a secret, but I had wheedled the complicated directions from the teen-age daughter of one of my neighbors. In those days you couldn't cross the river on the Swan Falls dam from the power house, so you had to drive in on dirt roads from the village of Murphy on the south side of the river. Murphy was famous for a time for having a single parking meter in front of the courthouse.

We zigzagged down a rocky dirt road between black basalt cliffs and gray green sagebrush. Across the river ahead, black basalt teeth lined the top of the canyon wall. At the bottom of the grade we met a truck and tractor and drove off the road to let them by. Margaret saw the tractor before I did. and drove her Volkswagen bus off the road in a flat place. As I drove off into the brush, I heard air hissing out of a tire. With the help of a couple of scouts I changed the tire. It never occurred to me that doing so would re-injure my back. I was in a hurry, for it was already 80 degrees. It would soon be too hot to get the boys to walk the two rough miles to the petroglyphs. The boys and Margaret helped me jack up the car and put on the spare, but I lifted the flat tire back into the car myself without thinking about it.

After changing the tire, we drove on to where the road was blocked off at an abandoned farmhouse. My back and leg had already begun to hurt again. We hiked the two miles to a field of big black boulders. The boulders are today known as melon gravel. They had been deposited by the Bonneville flood 15,000 years ago when the shore of ancient Lake Bonneville broke and sent a massive surge of water down the Snake River canyon. The petroglyphs cut into these rocks were of creatures with bug eyes and strange headdresses. The boys had more fun wading in a lagoon the ancients had constructed in the river and trying to catch the carp in it than they did looking at the petroglyphs. By then it must have been well over 100. I had Hilary and Stuart with me since I thought they'd enjoy going on the trip. On the way back to the car Stuart's freckled face turned so red I was afraid he was getting heat stroke. Without thinking how heavy he was I picked him up and set him in the river.

"What did you do that for?" Stuart said, his face turning even redder.

"You were getting too hot. I had to cool you off."

"You could have let me take off my jeans and shoes first!"

On the way home, Stuart dripped all over the car, but he suffered no ill effects from the heat. However, my back felt as though someone was pinching it .The next day the pain in my back and right leg was worse and its foot turned numb. When

I went to the doctor again, he thought I might have a slipped disk and scheduled me for a myelogram. It was a test where dye injected into the spinal cord shows up on X-rays. After the test, the gray-haired doctor brought a sheaf of X-rays into my hospital room, held up one above me, looked down through his bifocals and pointed, "This bright line is your spinal cord and that narrow place is where the disk is pressing on it. You need to have the bad part of the disk removed."

The doctor said I would be much more likely to be able to hike if I had the operation. Today a doctor would have told me to wait for it to heal on its own, My eyes filled with tears: I feared the injury would mean no hiking ever again. "You ll be able to do most things again afterwards," the doctor said to my relief.

"Will it get well if I don't have the surgery?"

"Probably not and your disk might push farther into the spinal cord."

The night before the operation I was terrified of waking up and finding myself paralyzed. It seemed hours before they came and took me to surgery, but it was actually only 10 a.m. When I told Wayne I needed the operation and planned to have it on June 6, he said, "I 'd like you to wait until after the Democratic convention. That's the 20th and 21st."

"The doctor is going on vacation, and after the operation I have to wait a month before I can go to the mountains. If I wait until July, the kids will have to go back to school before I can go to the cabin."

"I still wish you'd wait. Maybe you really don't need the operation after all and if you wait your back might get better by itself. I've got to be at that convention. Some of the delegates want to put support for Cesar Chavez and his lettuce boycott in California into the platform. That would really hurt candidates here, so I've got to be there to make sure it doesn't happen."

I went ahead and had the operation on June 6 anyway. I just had to be able to go to the mountains that summer. I remember little of the day of the operation, except asking Wayne if the operation was over and not believing it was because it seemed as though no time had passed. A few months later I learned that the doctor had been a pilot in the German Luftwaffe (air force) in World War II. That made me think that I hadn't needed the operation after all if the doctor was a Nazi. However, he was the only orthopedic doctor in Caldwell, then.

The surgery cost so much more than our insurance covered that Wayne decided that Leslie, who was 13, could take care of the younger kids while I was in the hospital. Doug, then sixteen, was working at a restaurant that summer, so he couldn't babysit. Wayne was close by and home at night until he went off to the Democratic Convention.

I called Leslie several times a day to see how the kids were getting along and to give her instructions. When Wayne brought me home after the convention that

Sunday evening, the kids had put up balloons and a welcome home sign and they had presents for me. Wayne gave me an umbrella so I could take walks in the rain. I thought Leslie had done a good job of taking care of the kids until I couldn't find any clean towels. When I asked her where the clean towels were, she said, "In the brown bathroom." She hurried outside and rode off on her bicycle. When I looked in the cupboards and closets I found her closet stuffed full of dirty clothes, sheets, and towels clear to its ceiling. I just put the towels in the washer and didn't say a word to Leslie about it. She had done an amazing job of keeping care of the kids and the house for a 13-year-old.

The doctor had told me that walking was the key to being able to hike again. I was determined to hike again so every day I walked farther, although the same leg that hurt before the surgery still hurt some. A week after the surgery I walked around the block three times. Within ten days I was able to clean the house, though it made my back ache and made me very tired. After two weeks I ran Stuart's fifth birthday party for six guests with only a little help from Leslie. By then I was able to walk two miles.

All my effort was worth it. A month after the surgery, the doctor said I could go to the mountains and try hiking, if I wore my back brace and didn't carry more than five pounds. Wayne went with us to the cabin to help the kids carry in all the luggage, food, and water and dig the hole for the toilet. On the way up we stopped to swim at Havens, a hot springs lodge near Lowman. Doug didn't go with us because by then he had a job clearing brush at the new scout camp at McCall. After the weekend, Wayne returned to work in Caldwell but came up on one weekend to see us. I felt very happy to be in the mountains after all the trauma with my back. The snowbank moose on Galena Peak across the valley, the sego lilies in bloom, and the happy smell of the pines and sagebrush made me feel like skipping if I had dared to.

Instead of hauling water from the creek in five gallon containers, each of which weighed 40 pounds, I used plastic gallon milk jugs that weighed only 8 pounds when full. It was easier to fill them from a faucet at one of the campgrounds at Alturas Lake than from the creek, so that is what we usually did. I had been saving jugs and by then had about thirty. One time some campers asked me where I was going with all the water jugs, the north pole? When I told them, they wanted to know why we were staying at a cabin that had no water.

In the three weeks we spent at the cabin, I took the kids on ten hikes. Now I can't believe I did that many so soon after my surgery. I wasn't afraid of falling and paralyzing myself. I just felt this huge wanting to go on hikes. I probably just needed to prove I still could.

On one of the first of these hikes, it had been only a little cloudy when we left the cabin. At Fallen Leaf it would cloud up for three days before it rained, so I didn't worry about rain. I planned to take the kids to the closest Alpine Creek Lake above Alturas Lake near our cabin. It was only 3 miles. We had walked only 1 mile before it began hailing. I put up our emergency tube tent and tried to start a fire. People had told me to take birthday candles to start a fire in wet weather, but they wouldn't light in the hailstorm. I didn't yet know about paraffin or jelly fire starters. The kids' sneakers were soaked and my boots were wet. It was just as cold in the tent as outside it, so we started back. The hail on the trail made it slippery. After ten minutes Stuart began to howl. Hilary was crying, too, but she only sobbed. About then we met a forest ranger in a yellow slicker. He was not someone we had met before and I was shivering too much to ask his name. He was rolling a wheel like one off a bicycle along the trail. I figured he was measuring the distance. He looked up and said, "What's the matter? Is he hurt?"

"No, we're fine," I said, "he's just cold. Our car is down at the trailhead." I hurried the kids past him. I didn't want to have to give the ranger my name and risk having him tell people I took my little kids on a hike in a hailstorm. By then so much hail had covered the trail it looked like snow.

As we passed, the ranger lifted one hand off the wheel and pointed toward the trailhead. He said, "Do you want me to go with you? I've got a thermos of coffee in the truck."

"No thanks," I said, "We'll be fine." It was only a mile farther, so I thought there was no danger. Later when I read about hypothermia, I realized that if one of us had fallen and been hurt we could have all died of it. I didn't know then that the Sawtooths have much more severe weather than the Sierras around Fallen Leaf. There, dying of cold had been called exposure and happened so seldom no one worried about it.

When it cleared up, I tried the same hike again. I found that there was no trail beyond the three mile point. I was determined to reach the lake anyway. We followed a faint path that petered out at the base of a waterfall.

The topo map showed we had to climb along the waterfall to reach the lake.

It was difficult getting Stuart and Hilary up it because their sneakers kept slipping on the pebbles but we made it to the lake. The lake was mostly surrounded by cliffs, including a high granite tower. It took us six hours from the trailhead to get there.

At lunch Neal, Hilary, and Stuart pulled stuffed toys out of their day packs instead of fishing poles. There was a bear, a Raggedy Ann and Andy and two small rabbits. While Leslie fished and I walked around the lake a ways, they made up a puppet show. When I came back they gave their show for me, using a flat boulder for a stage. On the hike back I stopped, in the big meadow, built a fire, and cooked a Lipton noodle dinner for the kids. I wanted to make sure they stayed warm and happy all the way to the car. Half the noodles fell in the fire but we had enough anyway.

Two days later we hiked to Ocalkens Lakes in the White Clouds. To get there, I drove to Stanley, then down the Salmon River toward Challis for 24 miles, and up Slate Creek for 8 miles to the end of the road at a mine. Here we saw a bulldozer running. We spent an hour floundering around in the woods beyond the mine trying to find the trail. Later I found out the trail had been discontinued by the Forest Service a few years earlier. As we looked a dog followed us around and scared Hilary.

When Leslie went over to the creek to look for the trail, she came back screaming, "There's a bear!"

We just couldn't be scared away from finding the trail by a bear, so I walked over to see. It turned out to be a steer and it just kept on eating grass. Soon after that we found the trail up on the hillside. Right away a man on horseback rode down the trail toward us. "Have you seen any cows? I'm missing three. My partner and I are driving 300 head over into Warm Springs Canyon."

Pointing, I said, "There's one."

It was a steep and rocky hike, but we made it all right. The kids were pleased they could see the tops of two of the white peaks, the ones Neal said were his white mountains.

Back at the cabin that night about midnight I heard footsteps on the porch, I thought it was a burglar, and screamed. I ran up the stairs to the loft to hide. My screaming had woken up Leslie, but no one else. She sat up in bed in her pink nightie and said, "What's the matter? Did you hurt yourself?"

"I heard footsteps on the porch. Someone's trying to break in."

"Did you look out the window to see who it was?"

"No, I was too scared."

"Why don't you look."

When I looked out her bedroom window, a black bear was walking down our driveway, and I felt very silly. When that bear came back a few days later, I knew the footsteps were not a prowler and we scared it away by thumping on the wall.

In early August all seven of us drove to Palo Alto and then to Fallen Leaf. We drove at night so the kids wouldn't fight. We hadn't told my parents we were going to do this, so when we arrived at 7 a.m. my mother was very surprised. In Palo Alto Wayne took my mother and the three older kids to Candlestick Park in South San Francisco to see the Giants play. I didn't want to sit in the bleachers with my tender back and I didn't think Hilary and Stuart could sit still for a baseball game. So I walked with them to the swimming pool in Rinconada Park a half block from my parents' house. Another day Wayne and my father went to the national Bar convention in San Francisco, while my mother and I drove the kids to the beach at Half Moon Bay, to walk in a redwoods park, and to Marine Land to see the killer whales perform. When Wayne and I returned from a Stanford lawyers dinner one evening, we found that my brother Tom had come over from his house at Pleasanton and borrowed Doug to help him build his cabin. His cabin site was at Kirkwood Meadows near the Carson Pass, 40 miles south of Lake Tahoe. He needed help lifting the roof timbers into place. (My sister Dodie had married a man, Pete Seagle, whose parents ran a music camp in the Adirondacks called the Seagle Colony. The camp had 17 cabins, all with pianos, a 200 year old farmhouse, and its own little lake, which they called the pond.)

At Fallen Leaf, Wayne wanted to climb Tallac the mountain I had climbed when I was six because he had heard so much about it over the years. My father also wanted to climb Tallac to see if he still could. He had had a lobe of one lung removed that winter because of lung cancer. He had never smoked, but for forty years had ridden in the smoking car of the train while commuting to San Francisco. That car was less crowded than the other cars so he could spread out his papers and get some work done on the train. Tallac was a 10 mile round trip and 3500 foot climb from the original trailhead at Glen Alpine. By 1972 it was a 12 mile round trip because by then the road was gated at Lily Lake.

We managed to reach the top of Tallac with all five kids and my dad although we had a few problems. Many wooden steps had been put in the trail since I had last hiked it 17 years before. Neal had to count them all, 429 of them, which made him slower. Then when we reached the shortcut above Gilmore Lake that cuts between long switchbacks, Neal said, "No. We need to stay on the trail. We'll get lost!"

"This is the way Grandpa always goes," I said, "He's climbed Tallac 100 times and he's never gotten lost."

"I don't care. I'm not going."

I wondered when he would outgrow his fear of letting lost.

Luckily the switchbacks led through wildflowers and sprawled whitebark pines so it was a pretty walk, even if longer. From this slope, we had a wide view of the four mountains called the Crystal Range above Desolation Valley. I had climbed them all in one day the first summer I worked at the Stanford Sierra Camp at Fallen Leaf. The other kids and Wayne hiked the shortcut with my father, while I took Neal the long way. From the top, Fallen Leaf looked like a blue boot print in a green shag rug, not like a leaf at all. The pale blue platter of Lake Tahoe had turned black at its southern edge from all the development, which by then had become a town called South Tahoe. This was long before a sewer system for the whole area was installed and turned the black water blue again.

Back in Caldwell at the end of August I continued walking five miles a day and doing exercises in hopes of being able to ski that winter. One day that fall as I walked along an irrigation ditch in the country outside Caldwell I gazed at the hazy line of mountains in the distance and thought back to the summer and all the hikes. I wondered what I would do that winter if I couldn't ski.

Hilary and Start starting up the Little Boulder Creek trail.

CHAPTER 11: BEGINNING A BOOK IN SECRET

What would I do that winter if I couldn't ski with the family? Sit in the lodge? I would need something besides the class I was taking toward a teaching credential. When I went to the library I saw a guidebook to the Cascades and that gave me the idea of writing one for the Sawtooths and White Clouds. I thought it would help people like me who had a hard time with unsigned trails and bad roads like Hell Roaring and 4th of July.

The book I found was *100 Hikes in Western Washington* by Louise Marshall. It had been published in 1966, two years before our cabin was built. At the top of each hike this book listed the round trip distance, elevation gain, difficulty, and the topographic maps needed. Then the first sentence or two described the beautiful things to see on the hike. That was exactly the kind of book I wanted to write for the Sawtooths and White Clouds.

Congress had just designated the Sawtooth, White Cloud, and Boulder Mountains as a National Recreation Area. The Sawtooth Mountains within it were already wilderness. Writing a guidebook would give me an excuse for spending more time hiking from our cabin, and that would be a lot of fun. It might also keep the kids interested in taking more hikes than they otherwise would want to do.

On the day Stuart started kindergarten I sat down at the dining table with some lined paper and drafted the beginning of one hike. Then I went down to the basement cupboard and got out Wayne's old typewriter and carried it upstairs. I undid the latch on the cardboard case and set the typewriter on my little maple desk. I had bought the desk for $50 when I was 14 and Aunt Nellie left me $100 in her will. The typewriter had the small elite type and it's ribbon wasn't new so it's print was faint. It was the only typewriter we had. The desk was against a wall with no windows so I couldn't look outdoors and get distracted. The robin's egg blue walls of the living room made me feel relaxed. I had only one more hour before I had to walk to the Methodist Church and get Stuart before Wayne came home for lunch.

Idaho didn't have public kindergartens so Stuart went to a private one. Even today only a few districts can afford to have public kindergartens. I didn't want Wayne to know about the guidebook because he was paying for me to take classes toward my teaching credential and expected me to teach. I didn't dare tell him I might want to write books instead. I was already worried about keeping order in the classroom because I had trouble making my own kids behave.

My book would have directions for the trails in the new Sawtooth National Recreation Area. Congress had just passed the legislation for it a few weeks before. It included the Sawtooth, Boulder, and White Cloud and some of the Smoky Mountains. These were the mountains surrounding our cabin. I hoped my book would help people like me prepare for the bad access roads to the traiheads. I also wanted it to help them find the secret routes to the most beautiful places like Saddleback Lakes.

As I typed and kept making mistakes I realized I should be putting in another load of laundry and folding the dry clothes. The dirty clothes were falling out of the clothes chute onto the utility room floor and I had to step over them to get to the half bath. But if I didn't start the book now when I had some time I was afraid I never would. So I kept on but went back to longhand because I didn't have to worry about mistakes. I would just type it later.

I made what I wrote just like the book on the Cascades that I had checked out of the library. I put all the things its author had used even the topographic maps at the beginning of each hike. Next I described the distinctive things hikers would see on that trail. I tried to describe the beauty of the lakes and surrounding mountains but it was difficult to make them sound unique.

I checked the elevation gains and distances with the topographic maps. New maps had just come out for part of the Sawtooths and White Clouds. I used the 40 foot contour lines on the maps to add up the elevation gains. When I had finished only two sentences of the description for the second hike it was time to go get Stuart. I took the papers and stuck them in my desk. Then I set off down the street and as I walked I wished it was still summer and I was hiking the trails I had been trying to describe.

Back home with Stuart I fixed soup and sandwiches for Wayne, Stuart, and myself. After lunch, Wayne drove back to the office and I left Stuart to play with his Legos and read the chapter in the language arts book that I needed to read before my class later that afternoon. After a few pages I heard a lot of splashing from the half bath.

When I went to see, I found Stuart had put our puppy, Trixie, in the toilet. He said, “I wanted to see if she’d go to the bathroom. Then we wouldn’t have to take her outside all the time.”

By the time he had helped me give Trixie a bath in the tub upstairs, and cleaned her black hairs out of the tub the other kids had come home and it was time for my class.

After class I took Leslie to a sale at Sears downtown. She wasn’t happy with her clothes and the school had just informed her that girls couldn’t wear jeans. One day that week she had hidden in her closet and not gone to school because she said she didn’t have anything to wear.

Each morning that fall I wrote in my book for at least an hour, but I still didn’t tell anyone what I was doing. I hid the pages on my closet shelf. By Christmas I had written up the 30 trails I had hiked in the four years since we had the cabin, and I wondered what I should do next with what I had written.

One day in March of 1973, when I went to my student teaching class at the College of Idaho I saw a poster. It advertised a book on six hikes in the Owyhees and six hikes in the Seven Devils. It had been published by something called the Snake River Regional Studies Center. A student had done the hikes and written the book as a work-study project. I found that the center was located at the college and went to see its director Donna Parsons, hoping the center might publish my book.

The office of the center was on the second floor of the biology building. It opened off a wide foyer with a glass cage in the middle. The cage contained a giant greenish-gray iguana. It lay there like a big blob of clay except for its tongue darting in and out. A woman came out of one of the offices and introduced herself as Donna Parsons and asked what I was doing there. Donna was a compact woman with glasses and shoulder length gray hair tied back at the nape of her neck. She led me into her small office where I showed her my manuscript, sketch maps, and a couple of photos. She said, “That’s a good idea for a book and the Sawtooths are in the drainage of the Snake River, so it fits with our purpose.”

She said she’d be glad to edit the manuscript and give me advice, but wasn’t sure the center had enough money to publish it. They had to get grants to publish the Owyhees book and the environmental education book she had written. “Let me show you."

She took me into a large closet next to her office that was lined with bookshelves. She pulled down an 8-by-11 inch book with a color cover. It was a guidebook for places in Idaho that were good for teaching kids about the environment. The title was *Idaho: An Outdoor Classroom*. It had been paid for by the U.S. Department of Education. The book described several loop drives and their plants, animals, geology, and landmarks.

"How old are your kids?" she asked.

When I told her they were 5, 7, 10, 13, and 16 she said, "You doing your book with your kids all still at home reminds me of when I was working on mine. I took the three of them on several camping trips. It was a lot of fun."

Donna had taught at Caldwell High School before taking a year off to write her book. She had become director of the Snake River Center two years earlier. The center was funded by a big non-profit as well as the college. Donna said she would show my manuscript to her board and see what they thought.

After I saw Donna I was so encouraged I finally told Wayne about my book. He said, "I already know about it. Leslie told me you were writing something and keeping it on your closet shelf. Why didn't you tell me before?"

"I didn't want you to think I was wasting my time when I have so many other things to do."

"It's not a waste of time. A book of trail directions will be very useful to a lot of people."

Two weeks later Donna called and said the committee was enthused about it and that I should come see her again. She said I needed to write an introduction and draw better maps. In the meantime she would edit it. Then she would write a letter to go with the introduction and sample chapters and I should send this out to publishers. There were at least 40 publishers she knew about.

In early June of 1973, Wayne went up to the cabin to meet his brother, Bruce, and the lumberyard carpenter to install the Franklin stove. We had ordered the stove from Montgomery Ward and brought it to the cabin two years earlier. Wayne and Bruce and the carpenter had a lot of trouble getting the parts put together but they finally got it all done. The stove was wide and black with folding doors in front of the firebox. Two brass balls decorated the front corners and a black stovepipe connected near the roof with an insulated silver chimney. By then the cabin had a front deck and green shutters on the windows. Inside we had stairs to the loft, wiring, and the chipboard floors had been varnished. Even though it was the middle of June it snowed two inches that night, so the stove's heat was wonderful.

The next day my parents came from California to visit. They stayed as usual at

Swiss Villa, the motel in Obsidian. My parents only wanted to go on hikes I had already done, but I was finally able to persuade them to go on one hike for the book. The kids and I went with them to Crater Lake up Slate Creek in the White Clouds. It was an 8-mile round trip. My mother hiked only about half way, but my kids were inspired by Grandpa and kept up with him. My father was fascinated by some old mining buildings on the lake shore and took pictures of us looking out of them. They all fell down a couple of years later.

After my parents left for home, I tried to add more hikes for the book. The first one I did was to Goat Lake in the Sawtooths. I went with Judy Kepner, a woman I had met on the Alturas Lake beach. I met her when her twins, Eric and Wendy who were seven, started playing with Hilary and Stuart. Judy and her children were staying with her parents in their cabin near Pettit Lake. It was on the flats below Pettit Lake and was one of the cabins removed by the Forest Service a few years later. Judy's parents took care of the twins and Hilary and Stuart at their cabin during the hike.

Judy and I and her dog, Blue, started out at Iron Creek, the trailhead for Sawtooth Lake north of Stanley. After a mile we turned south on the Alpine Way Trail. It goes 10 miles or so to Redfish from there. Two miles along it we turned off on an unmarked side trail to Goat Falls as the chief wilderness ranger, Dave Lee, had told me to do. He had said just to go to the waterfall and climb up it. At the creek that came down from the waterfall we stopped and looked for a way up. It was all cliffs.

Judy, and Blue, stopped beside me. The dog was an Australian shepherd and was called Blue because his back was blue-gray with black spots. He licked my hand and I felt his panting.

"Is this the way the ranger told you to go?"

I squinted up at the spray. "He said just to go up the waterfall."

Blue began to scramble up the granite slabs at the edge of the falls.

"Stay!" Judy called, but he kept going up the near vertical slope and disappeared.

"What do you want to do?" I asked. Several people had talked about going to Goat Lake, so I felt I had to put it in the guidebook. I stared at the cliffs, wondering what to do.

Then Blue came leaping down the slabs with a clatter. "Whuf, whuf!" He panted and put his paws on Judy s thighs, nearly knocking her over. I reached out to steady her.

Short and dark-haired, with a smattering of freckles, she wasn't much taller than Blue when he stood on his hind feet.

"He's found a way up. Let's just follow him."

“Go,” she said and Blue scrambled up the slabs and out of sight again.

Pulling ourselves up with branches and testing each footstep, we followed. Blue came back if we didn’t come right up after him. Following him, we could see which cliff, or crack or steep dirt slope to climb. After about 150 feet of near vertical climbing the slope lessened. Now there were scratchy bushes to fight our way through as well as slippery pebbles on the ground. The air was damp from the spray and smelled like dead pine needles.

“Good thing we didn’t bring the kids,” Judy yelled over the roar of the waterfall.

“Yeah. They couldn’t have gotten up this.”

I tried to imagine six year old Stuart and eight year old Hilary climbing the cliffs. They couldn’t reach far enough and Judy’s twins were even smaller.

After 20 minutes or so, the slope leveled and we saw Goat Lake ahead. At the lake, teal blue water held the reflections of two vertical snowbanks with pale turquoise crevices. Above them a wall of dark cliffs cast a shadow over the water, turning it navy blue.

Now we had to cross the creek, for ahead on our side was a steep slope of boulders. We teetered across the creek on rocks and a log to a granite outcrop shaded by whitebark pines. Below us at the edge of the lake two small boys were fishing. One of the boys turned and smiled at us.

“How old are you?” I asked “How on earth did you get up here?”

“I just went up the path. I’m seven.”

“Path. What path?”

The boy pointed his fishing pole across the creek downstream from where we had crossed it. “Over there by that big log.”

I could see a faint path where he pointed. We could have brought the kids after all. Dave Lee shouldn’t have kept the path a secret.

I hoped the rest of the hikes I had planned to add that summer weren’t going to be as difficult as this one or I wouldn’t be likely to get them done.

I was delighted that Judy and I were able to reach Goat Lake. It was already July 20. I hadn’t been able to persuade Wayne to take a family pack trip that would be useful for the book. Instead we were going to Banff and Jasper with a rented 16-foot camping trailer. I was eager to see those parks, but the trip would leave me no more time for book hikes before school started. It started the fourth week in August, with registration required the third week. This seemed to me unfair. It took too much of the best part of the summer.

After eating lunch on the outcrop, we followed the boy's path down beside the waterfall to the trail. On the way we met a professional photographer taking photos for a book on Idaho to be sponsored by one of the Idaho banks. One of his photos, a close up of a section of the waterfall, is in that book but not the lake. Judy and I followed the path back down to the unofficial trail. The path skirted most of the bushes and cliffs 20 or 30 feet from the waterfall. Near the bottom, it zigzagged across a steep open slope where we could see the trail below but the path we were following was so faint you wouldn't notice it from below unless you knew it was there.

The next hike I took for the book that summer was even harder. It was a backpacking trip on the east side of the White Clouds with Hilary and Stuart. I had to be able to backpack to finish the book, and I didn't know whether I could after the back operation of the summer before. I planned a three-day trip to get close to Castle Peak. I felt it was essential to include the area around Castle Peak because it was the site of the controversy three years earlier about ASARCO (American Smelting and Refining Company) putting a heap-leach molybdenum mine right under the face of the mountain. The controversy had led to Cecil Andrus' election as governor in 1970 and to the formation of the Sawtooth National Recreation Area in 1972.

For the trip, two days after Goat Lake I started driving from our cabin at 5:00 a.m. with Hilary and Stuart still in their pajamas. To reach the trailhead I had to drive 20 miles north to Stanley, 27 miles east of Stanley along the Salmon River and 20 miles south up the East Fork of the Salmon. When the kids woke up, we stopped at a campground for breakfast and for the kids to get dressed. I also had to put on my back brace. The doctor had told me to wear it whenever I did anything strenuous. I hadn't told him I planned to carry a pack.

Hilary poured cornflakes into paper bowls for us and then looked in the cooler. She looked up and said, "There isn't any milk like you said there would be."

I could see the milk carton still sitting in the refrigerator back at the cabin. "I'll mix up some Tang. We can have that in the cornflakes."

"Yuck! I'm not having Tang on my cornflakes! I want Oreos. There's Oreos in our lunches!" said Stuart.

I got out the Oreos and we ate them and drank Tang. As we drove up the East Fork the pleated face of Castle Peak soon appeared. Snow filled two slanting chimneys on its face making them look like giant claw marks. The road wound along through pastures and cottonwoods below sagebrush and reddish brown outcrops. For about 12 miles it was paved, then gravel, then rocky dirt with boulders. It is a much smoother road now but then I was afraid of getting stuck or having a flat tire.

It was 8:00 a.m. before we reached the Little Boulder Creek trailhead where our hike began. By then sunlight had crept down the ridges to the chocolate colored outcrops and awakened the astringent smell of the sagebrush. Except for cottonwoods along the East Fork, there were no trees at the trailhead, just sagebrush and rocks. Tingles of fear ran down my back at the prospect of sleeping out in the woods for two nights with only Hilary and Stuart for company. I also worried about one of us falling and breaking a leg and about murderers and hungry cougars.

Hilary and Stuart wore their first pairs of hiking boots, cheap ones of split leather. They carried orange nylon knapsacks with a change of clothes, a jacket and a rain poncho apiece, and a little of our food. To save weight we took only one fish pole and reel. With the help of my back brace I carried two sleeping bags, a kettle, the rest of the food, and a yellow plastic tube tent. One of the sleeping bags was Wayne's old rectangular one. I had unzipped it and safety-pinned it along one side so one child could sleep at each end.

The trail began in sagebrush across the road from a pit toilet and small parking areas. Today's transfer camp for the trail had not yet been built.

At first, Hilary and Stuart went so fast I dropped behind them, watching their orange packs, Stuart's yellow hat and Hilary's red and white hat bounce along. Along the trail I noticed pieces of pink facial tissue. I started to pick them up, thinking they were litter, but I discovered they were actually wilted flowers. Among the pink tissue were big white flowers, some with a pink tinge. Later I found in my flower book that they were evening primrose.

There was no shade, so the kids stopped to drink from their plastic water bottles and I soon caught up with them. Within a half hour Stuart reached up, pulled on my pack and said, "My pack is killing my shoulders."

He took it off and dragged it along by the straps, raising so much dust I found it hard to breathe. "Oh-oh," I thought and wondered if this trip was going to work out at all.

As Hilary and I waited for him, she rubbed her stomach and said, "I'm starving. Can we have some M&M's?"

"We ll have a snack at the first trees. If we stop sooner, it'll be too hot." I showed her the first green spot on the topographic map. Then I picked up Stuart's pack and carried it in one hand. "Come on. I'll tell you a story," I said.

I began a new story about David and Rachel. In the past, Hilary and Stuart had loved my stories about these imaginary children at Sawtooth City, a ghost town of log ruins about eight miles from our cabin. The town had flourished in the early 1880s after the owners of one of the mines built a toll road over Galena Summit to Ketchum.

"That's a stupid story." said Stuart, scowling and putting two dusty fingers in his mouth. "Tell Babar."

"You're carrying Stuart's pack. That's no fair. Mine hurts too." said Hilary, dropping hers.

“OK I’ll carry both packs and tell a Babar story if you walk right along. Once we reach the trees and we’ve had our snack, you must carry the packs yourselves.” I was afraid we’d soon have to turn around. As it was, carrying both packs in my hands made a sliver of pain run down one leg. I made up my own Babar stories, instead of using the ones in the books. The one today was about Babar’s giant shopping bag and all the things his kids put in it.

At the first Douglas firs about a mile up, we sank down into welcome shade. Here we drank from our water bottles, and ate M&M’s and beef jerky. Below us Little Boulder Creek hummed a cooling song.

To entertain the kids while they rested I pointed out the three mouse-like tails under each scale of the Douglas fir cones. I showed them how to make mustaches with some yellow green lichen by putting a piece of it under their noses and pouting. Hilary and Stuart couldn’t keep from laughing so their mustaches fell off. For a few minutes the mustaches made them forget how hard the hiking was.

When I insisted we go on, Stuart said, “It’s too hot. Can’t we just camp here?”

“No, it’s not far enough.” I stood up, put on my pack and started walking and telling another Babar story. As we struggled up the trail, I also pointed out wildflowers and then started a game of 20 questions. Whenever the trail changed direction or crossed a stream I stopped and wrote the change in a little red spiral notebook I carried in one hand. At 4 p.m. we reached a split in the trail. A sign read Castle Divide ahead and Livingston Mill, Willow Lake to the right. At the junction it was level enough to camp but cow pies littered the grass and cows wandered through the willows, their bells clanging.

Up the canyon from the junction rose Castle Peak and its neighbor. The dark gray face with snow chimneys was on the left and a picket fence of pale orange towers composed another mountain on the right. I later learned it is called Merriam Peak.

The kids helped me set up our yellow plastic tube tent and lay the sleeping bags in it. Then Hilary took the fishing pole to the lake and Stuart drew a town with charcoal on an outcrop for the little cars he had brought. I wandered around taking pictures of the two orange towers that peered over the ridge like pointed ears.

My sleeping bag idea for the kids didn’t work out as well as I expected. “He’s kicking me,” Hilary said, only a minute after she and Stuart had climbed into either end of the pinned-together sleeping bag.

“That’s because her feet are in my way,” said Stuart, sitting up again. “Make her move over.”

It took several minutes and a few bedtime songs such as *Down at the Station*, see the puffer bellies all in a row, before the kids settled down.

Even then, it was hours before I fell asleep that night. Every little breeze rattled the tent, making me peek out. I checked the shadows for cougars and bears. The creek sounded like motorcycles so I checked for them, too. As I lay there sleepless I wondered how I was ever going to get all the hikes done for the book. It was so hard to do even one of the longer ones with Hilary and Stuart. I lay awake for hours, wondering if daylight was ever going to come.

The next morning I put crackers and squeezy cheese, dried apricots, oreos, and M&M's in a baggie for lunch. Then we started out to see the rest of the Boulder Chain Lakes. I was relieved to find a young couple camped at the next lake, a mile above Willow. This lake, now called Hatchet, was close to the tower with two pointed ears. The fact that the lakes were close together made it easier to persuade the kids to walk along. We stopped for a long time at the fifth lake because it had a beach of orange sand. Across from the beach a row of orange towers shed rocks and pebbles into the water. Hilary and Stuart took off their boots and socks and used our cooking pot to mold a sand castle. I wiggled my toes in the sand, relishing their freedom from my boots.

Beyond the fifth lake there was a mile-long gap and then four more lakes clustered together. I was afraid it would be hard to get the kids up the lakeless section, but Hilary started making up her own Babar stories and that helped. We managed to reach the ninth lake, now called Scoop, the highest one on the trail. The trail climbed on a few hundred yards to a plateau, but I didn't bother with that. On the way down we stopped at the eighth lake for Hilary to fish.

Half way back to the fifth lake, Stuart and I had a nice long rest when Hilary realized she had forgotten the fish she had just caught. She insisted on going back for it. When we got back to camp, Hilary continued fishing and Stuart played with his cars in their charcoal and granite city. I sat beside the tent making notes and when I looked across the inlet to check on Hilary I couldn't see her at first. Then I realized she was lying on the ground. I hurried over and found her sobbing beside her stringer with four or five fish. "These fishies um all dead and they won't see their mommies and daddies any more."

What a tender-hearted little girl! When I cooked her fish by standing them on their heads in our little cooking pot and steaming them, she wouldn't eat any. I slept a little better that night because I knew the young couple were at the next lake,

I planned to hike to Castle Lake before going back to the car the next day. I was eager to put it in the book because Leslie had hiked to it with her environmental education group the summer before. She had said it was as beautiful as Saddleback lakes in the Sawtooths. Others I knew had been there as well. To reach Castle Lake we first hiked back to the junction in the cow meadow where we hid our packs in the willows. Then we took the uphill trail toward Castle Divide. After a mile we turned onto the side trail to Baker Lake, which Leslie had told me about. The lake was a small green lake in marsh grass under the dark gray face of Castle Peak and the apricot spindles of Merriam Peak. Along the shore was a string of A-frame cabins and a silver house trailer but no people. We didn't see any trail to Castle Lake, so we went back out to the main trail and climbed towards Castle Divide. I looked for the big flat place that Leslie said marked the turnoff to the last part of the trail to Castle Lake but we didn't see it. We saw only what looked like a goat path high up on white talus on the other side of the canyon. Hilary glared at me. "Where's the trail to the lake? I thought you said this wouldn't be a wild goose chase!"

"We're tired of wild goose chases, Mom," said Stuart, trying to pull me back down the trail.

At this I swore to myself and let the kids lead me back to Baker Lake. This time the caretakers for the mine buildings greeted us. The bearded, dark-haired geologist explained how to reach Castle Lake by a little mine road on the other side of a bridge over the outlet. I hadn't noticed a road or bridge there earlier. He said the road led to the prospect, and from it a path went to the big flat place that Leslie had mentioned. The goat path on the white talus was the trail to the lake.

The woman who wore granny glasses and her hair in a single braid offered to take care of Hilary and Stuart while I went to Castle Lake, but I turned her down. The kids and I were tired, the woman looked a little strange, and we had eaten all our food. Reluctantly, I turned and began the seven miles back to the trailhead. I needed Hilary and Stuart's enthusiasm for future trips and didn't want to push my luck with them. I was lucky to have covered as much ground with them as I had and to have found that I could backpack again in spite of my back operation.

As we descended, the thought of Castle Lake began to prick my mind like a big thorn. Although my thighs and shoulders ached I said, "Let's go back. I need to put Castle Lake in my book."

"No, Mom," Hilary stepped in front of me and put her arms out to each side of the trail as a barrier. "You said we're going back to the cabin and we're tired."

"You're right, we are," I sighed and turned around again.

I did six more hikes for the book during the ten days before our Canadian trip, but they were just day hikes. I was able to do so many hikes because Marie Osborn's daughter Melinda was willing to babysit. Marie, a nurse practitioner, had just started the Stanley clinic the year before. Since we didn't have a phone at our cabin Marie insisted I bring the kids to their cabin above Fisher Creek. I did four hikes in five days and then took Hilary and Stuart on an easy hike to Bridalveil Falls near Stanley Lake. On that hike the kids read comic books as they walked along,

Think Sun sign in the Bighorn Crags.

CHAPTER 12: THE BIGHORN CRAGS AND CASTLE LAKE

A few days after school started in 1973, a rural district, Wilder, near Caldwell, hired me to teach a 6th grade overflow class as a temporary teacher. The town had a main street, a few houses and a labor camp of cinder block cabins. The school had been constructed on such a limited budget that the supply closet served as the place to make the teachers' coffee, and a closet tacked on to the end of my classroom was the principal's office. Lesson plans and grading papers made teaching a lot more work than I had expected. I had to keep my students in order and couldn't. Because of this I soon began to hate teaching.

The week school started Donna Parsons called and asked me to submit a finished manuscript to her for the Regional Studies Center to consider again for publishing. I had no time to type the new hikes I had done for it, so I paid Wayne s secretary. Mary Alley, to type it for me. Donna said my maps weren't good enough and suggested I have them drawn professionally. Even if I could have found someone, it would be too expensive. So I drew new maps with felt pens on Mylar, a frosted plastic used for engineering drawings.

I was glad the school didn't need me after the migrant children left for Texas in December. After that I just substituted in various school; districts. Substituting was even more difficult than the temporary teaching. After a fifth grade boy threw a baseball at his teacher's 20 gallon aquarium and broke it with a resulting flood, I often sneaked the upstairs telephone off the hook in the early mornings so no school could call me. Wayne couldn't see why I couldn't find a permanent job. I could, though. I still had five children at home and the superintendents probably felt I couldn't manage a job, too. Also at that time there was an oversupply of teachers.

I was surprised the next spring when Wayne said, "I'd like to go on a pack trip this summer. Doug's going off to college in the fall, It's probably our last chance to take another trip with the whole family."

"Can we go to Spangle Lakes in the Sawtooths?" I asked, "I need those lakes in my book."

"I want to go to the Big Horn Crags up in the Idaho Primitive Area. A scoutmaster in Nampa said it has beautiful rock towers and excellent fishing."

I was disappointed the trip would not add any trails to my book, but I was pleased that Wayne wanted to go on another pack trip. He arranged with a Challis packer Albert Lamper, to carry in our food and gear eight miles to Birdbill Lake. Wayne planned that we would carry the stuff out ourselves after we ate up the food.

To begin the trip, we drove 80 miles from our cabin to Challis. By then we had a bigger car, a 1969 GMC Suburban we had bought from one of Wayne's law partners. From Challis we drove 55 miles on rough dirt roads to the main trailhead at Crags Campground. The Bighorn Crags are just southeast of the confluence of the Middle Fork and main Salmon rivers. On the way, we had a flat tire, but we made it to the end of the road. The last 3 miles were so rough and steep we saw a few cars just left at the side of the road. We camped the first night at our packer's base camp in his guest tepees. The next day we hiked in to the lake, detouring around snowfields and the towers of Fishfin Ridge. This ridge resembled a gigantic prehistoric fish. Mr. Lamper brought in his horses by a detour that avoided the snowbanks. Above magenta shooting stars on the lake shore rose the immense tooth of the head of Fishfin Ridge, which was called Knuckle Peak.

As soon as the horses were unloaded, it began to rain and it rained every day except one. Wayne and I had a nylon backpacking tent that I had just sewed from a Frostline kit, but the kids just had plastic tube tents. The rainwater ran in one end of those tents and out the other. By then I had sewed Frostline sleeping bags for the whole family. The second afternoon the thunderstorm was so bad all seven of us took refuge in the nylon tent for more than an hour. Thunder crashing less than a second away and hail drumming on the tent was so loud the kids had trouble hearing me reading from Agatha Christie.

When the rain stopped at twilight, Wayne started a fire for soup and cocoa. As he rubbed citronella on his face to keep off the mosquitoes, he sighed and said, "I think we should just hike out tomorrow. The kid's tents are no good."

"We paid to bring in all this stuff. We can't carry it out until we eat up the food."

"Oh yes we can Doug and I can."

Now that we were here I wanted to finish the trip. The Crags were more spectacular than I had expected. "Can't we at least wait a couple of days and see if it clears up?"

"It may not be worth it. I don't want everybody to be miserable," Wayne said, and blew on the smouldering fire.

The morning after the thunderstorm, the rain stopped for awhile, so we stayed. Neal built a "think sun" sign with sticks and lime green lichen and asked us to do a "sun dance" around it. He danced around the sign, his hair falling over his face as he bent forward and back yelling in a war whoop. He pulled each of us up saying "Come on. The more people who dance, the better it will work." Trying to keep from laughing, we all danced. To my surprise, the next day was the only day of the trip it didn't rain. That day we hiked four miles to the largest lake, Ship Island, and saw its tree-masted island. From the far end of the lake, we looked down cliffs toward the Middle Fork of the Salmon River. We had to hang onto Stuart who kept trying to get down far enough to see the river. We took two more day hikes in the rain and then backpacked 2 miles back toward the trailhead and over to Wilson Lake to make the hike out shorter. On our day hike to Big Clear Lake we found a campsite with a tree that had been splintered by the lightning into four-foot pieces. I felt lucky that hadn't happened in our campsite.

On our last night at Wilson Lake, I photographed the kids in their soggy down jackets, shielding the camera from the rain with a corner of my poncho. After supper, we sat around the fire, singing songs, telling stories, and acting silly. Pitch and grime

DO Lee Peak from Walker Lake in the White Clouds

covered my hands, my clothes were damp, my scalp itched, and the smell of citronella stung my nose.

At sunset, mist like pink cotton-candy rolled up the canyon. Wiping the water dripping off the end of my nose with the back of my hand, I said, “Red sky at night means it’s going to clear up, and we’re leaving tomorrow. That figures.”

“Aw, Mom, doesn’t matter,” said Doug. “We had a good time anyhow. If it hadn’t rained, we wouldn’t have had anything to do: no trenches to dig, no stuff to dry, no excitement.”

I looked at Wayne and grinned. It really had been fun in spite of the rain. The book could wait.

After the Bighorn Crags trip, Leslie, Wayne and Doug returned to Caldwell to work but the three younger kids stayed up at the cabin with me for another week to help with hikes for the book. To spark their enthusiasm I let them choose the hikes. They had wanted to see Neal’s white mountains in the White Clouds up close, but the closest we’d come was Antz Basin on the way to Born Lakes. The white mountains, an eight mile long section of the White Clouds called the White Cloud Peaks are made of metamorphic rock. Some say it is marble, others quartzite, and a few say it is halfway in between. I figured the closest we could come to these peaks was on the other side of them, the east side, at the Big Boulder Lakes. Of course I wanted to add the Big Boulders to my book.

To reach the trailhead for the Big Boulders, we drove east of Stanley along the Salmon River, then south up its East Fork and west up a side road to the old Livingston Mill. The mine was located by A.S. and W.S. Livingston in 1882 and they shipped ore by pack train. Later owners built a road without permission from the Forest Service, by starting at the mine and working down to the East Fork. The mill and several brown cabins with tin roofs stood in a basin of sagebrush and Douglas fir below stacks of cliffs that looked like chocolate layer cakes.

It was seven steep miles through sagebrush that perfumed us with its smell to Walker Lake where we camped. To keep Hilary and Stuart walking I again told stories about David and Rachel who lived at Sawtooth City. Hilary and Stuart by then had frame packs with padded waistbands. The packs were a lot more comfortable than the knapsacks they had before. Neal’s shoulder length hair and shapeless gray felt hat added to his grungy appearance. Wires of dark gold hair stuck out from Hilary s long braids. Stuart’s curls were topped with a dirty white baseball cap that said Dannon. He had won it in a cross-country ski race.

When we reached Walker Lake, we saw only orange and gray mountains, not white. But I figured it was the wrong time of day for them to be white. From our cabin they were white only in the afternoon. Once we had set up the tent, we left our packs and started for the Big Boulder Lakes. The map showed they were right under what I thought were the white peaks. Luckily, some other hikers at Walker Lake described a cross-country route. Their way went up a side creek into a flat valley covered with wildflowers and then up a path over pebbles and ledges to a narrow lake called Hook. From there it was only a short up and down over granite outcrops to Cove Lake, the first of the three Big Boulder Lakes.

That lake shone like cobalt glass among white granite peninsulas. Between the peninsulas, gentians grew on little mounds of grass called frost hummocks, which had been pushed up by needles of ice. Behind the lakes, a pearl-gray ridge with pale stripes and a pointed end blended into the overcast sky. I figured from the map that the ridge had to be Neal's white mountains, and they would be white in the morning.

As we approached Cove Lake, Hilary pointed to the mountain wall and said "Neal your white mountains are saying Hi!"

Indeed the cracks and shadows did spell out that word. As we walked around the second lake, Hilary flopped down on a boulder. "I don't want to go to the third lake. I'm tired." Her face was sunburned and dusty, and her blue sweater had a big patch of spilled cocoa.

Cirque Lake was only a half mile farther and 150 feet higher. We had come so far, and I needed to include all three Big Boulder Lakes in the book. I gave Hilary a granola bar and left her there with her paperback book, *Pippi Longstocking*. I figured she would be safe enough because we would be so close. The boys and I climbed the inlet to the lake, which had milky aquamarine water, a few dwarfed whitebark pines, and alpine plants. Above it, talus gave way to dusty, cracked snow below the striped cliffs.

Castle Lake

Stuart pushed up his hat, looked up at the cliffs and said, "Those aren't Neal's white mountains. They aren't white."

"Remember, from our cabin the white mountains only look white in the afternoon," I said. "We re on the other side now, so they would look white in the morning instead."

While Neal fished, Stuart collected bits of the white rock, and I took pictures. Then rocks rattled and Hilary appeared.

It was hard to sleep that night with four people in three sleeping bags in our two-person tent, but we managed. As soon as the sun came up at Walker Lake the next morning, I left the kids asleep and climbed a low ridge above camp to make sure the mountains just above the Boulder Lakes were the right ones. The ridge above the Big Boulder Lakes glowed white in the morning sun like a gigantic bar of light. At that time the highest point was sometimes called Alabaster Prak, but today the tallest white mountain with the stripes is named D.O. Lee Peak, after Dave Lee, the first wilderness ranger in the SNRA.

A few days later when I returned to Caldwell, Donna called me and said the Regional Studies board had decided they didn't have the money to publish my book. She insisted that instead I send letters to the list of 40 publishers she had researched. "You write a letter telling about the book, and I'll write a letter recommending it from the Snake River Studies Center," she said. After we sent the letters, only three of the publishers wanted to read the manuscript, and after they did, none wanted to publish it. Donna just shrugged and said, "It's not your writing, it's that Idaho has less than a million people. There are more publishers. There's one in Colorado that wasn't on our list. Let's try them."

She also said I should write the Sawtooth National Recreation Area to ask one of the rangers to edit the manuscript for accuracy. When I didn't receive an answer to my letter, I called and spoke to the assistant to the First Chief Wlderness Ranger. He said, "No, no one here has the time. There are already too many guidebooks, and we see no need for another."

What guidebooks? I thought there weren't any in the whole state except for the Regional Studies booklet on the Seven Devils and the Owyhees. A month or so later in the one bookstore there was then in Boise, I saw a little book called *Hiking Around Sun Valley* by Clarice Blechman. It contained only 19 hikes in the Sawtooth National Recreation Area. I thought it was funny. The rangers thought 19 hikes were too many. By then my manuscript contained more than 50 hikes, and would eventually have 73. (Today the sixth edition has 143.)

I also found a booklet in the library called *Mountain Lakes of Idaho* that had been published by the Idaho Department of Fish and Game. They had just put out an 8th edition. It gave only the general location, the number of acres, the kind of fish, and one phrase about each lake, such as no trail or rainbows to 10 inches It didn't tell how to reach the lake if there was no trail, or even where any of the trails started.

After the kids had all registered for school the third week in August of 1974, I decided to try to go to Castle Lake by myself. I was still determined to put that lake in my book. I had never backpacked alone, but I didn't think I could get Hilary and Stuart to go on another trip to look for Castle Lake. Wayne agreed to take care of them and the other kids, or at least I thought he did. I felt I just had to put that hike in the book because Castle Lake was just above the site of the proposed molybdenum mine that had caused so much controversy in 1970.

The afternoon before the hike I drove up to the cabin and stayed overnight, but didn't sleep much. I tried to sleep in my sleeping bag but it was too hot, and I hadn't brought any sheets for the bed. Also, every creak of the roof, as it cooled with the night, sounded like a footstep. To cover as much new ground as possible I hiked in from Fourth of July Creek instead of from the East Fork of the Salmon. Just driving the boulder-filled Fourth of July road by myself was scary. Then at the trailhead, I ran over a piece of glass I didn't see, and a tire hissed flat. Lifting the spare tire out and putting the flat tire back in the car might re-injure my back, so I just hiked off and left the tire flat. My pack weighed only 20 pounds. I carried a plastic tube tent, matches, two topographic maps, a one-quart pot, a poncho, a sweater, a woolly hat, a sleeping bag, some food, and a thin four foot long foam pad. If it had snowed as it can the end of August in those mountains I would have been in trouble.

I hiked to Fourth of July lake, over a little divide to Washington Lake, down the canyon of Washington Creek and up to Chamberlain Divide, six miles from my car. Here I could see the whole face of Castle Peak, the highest mountain in the SNRA. The left half of the mountain was orange and gray pleated rock but the right half looked as though it had been sprayed with whipped cream. It was such a beautiful and strange view I felt as though I had hiked off the edge of the earth onto another planet.

From the lowest of the Chamberlain Lakes in the basin below the peak, the trail zigzagged up a white ridge to 10,000-foot Castle Divide. The farther I hiked from Fourth of July Creek the more worried I became about falling and breaking a leg. I had seen no one since I had started out that morning. From Castle Divide, I descended the trail I had hiked with Hilary and Stuart the year before while looking for Castle Lake. The route I had learned about on that trip started at Baker Lake, so I walked all the way down there, which was ten miles from Fourth of July Creek. I hoped the caretakers were still there and could remind me how to find Castle Lake. I walked through the lodgepoles past four or five A-frame cabins to an aluminum trailer house. From the doorway of the trailer a new caretaker, with faded blonde hair and wire-rimmed glasses, gave me the directions. Then she said, "We've got lots of cabins here. You're welcome to stay in one of them and have dinner with us."

"No thanks," I said, eager to get to Castle Lake, to see it at last. I first climbed the jeep road to ASARCO's abandoned mining prospect and then followed a path to the little valley Leslie had called the "big flat place." From there I crept along the "goat path" over a hill of slippery white talus and scree. My feet sent pieces of rock pattering down into the canyon.

As I descended to the lake I walked into the great shadow cast by the peak. From the shore charcoal-gray cliffs rose 2,000 feet into a violet-blue sky. Two snow-filled chimneys curved toward each other forming tall cartoon eyes above a smiling mouth of snow. As I walked around the lake looking for a campsite, I found a peninsula hiding a lagoon. The shadow had not yet hit its glowing turquoise water. It was so beautiful I felt I had to tiptoe.

Between granite knolls at the edge of the lagoon I set up the plastic tube tent under a whitebark pine. I had thought the Frostline tent way too heavy for me to carry. The whitebark's purple cones gave the place the wonderful odor of pine pitch. A gray and white Clark's nutcracker squawked from a nearby tree. I built a tiny fire and heated water for packaged stroganoff from the grocery store. Freeze dry food was too expensive for me then. After eating, I had nothing to do but listen to the wind rattle the plastic of the tent. The lake was already too shadowed for photographs, and I hadn't thought to bring a book to read. When the wind picked up I zipped myself into my sleeping bag, but the flapping tent snapped as loud as the flag at the ranger station. As the shadows crept closer, I began to imagine bears and cougars in every one. I decided to go back to Baker Lake so I could sleep. If I didn't get any sleep I wouldn't be able to hike out and drive back to Caldwell the next day. If I wasn't there I wouldn't be able to get the kids up for school. I packed up and scurried back to Baker Lake, reaching it just at dark.

The woman caretaker, Teresa, chuckled and said, "I told you, you should just have stayed here." Then she invited me inside their trailer for supper, but I just had a piece of Jello cheesecake, since I had already eaten. She told me her husband would soon be back from fishing and would want to talk to me.

After I finished the cheesecake Teresa and I played cribbage, although I hadn't played since I was a child. Then my grandma Ola's gentleman caller had taught me, because grandma didn't play cards.

When Teresa's husband, Mike, came back he suggested I make a side trip to nearby Noisy and Quiet lakes before starting back. He said there was a path that wasn't hard to follow. These lakes were good-sized but weren't labeled on the map.

I spent the night in a dilapidated cabin with four cots in it, but I still couldn't sleep. Mice skittered around in the walls and now and then across the floor. Before dawn I left my backpack in the cabin and started for Noisy and Quiet lakes, with only the map, my rain poncho, camera, water bottle, and four cookies. The track was a little sketchy but it wasn't hard to follow with the topographic map. Waterfalls rushed down the cliffs above one side of Noisy Lake, The waterfalls were hidden in the shadows but were loud and roaring. I reached Quiet Lake just as the sun hit the north side of Castle Peak, bringing out the interlocking triangles that were created by avalanche chutes. I was glad I had hiked the extra miles, for the route to it and Noisy Lake would make a splendid addition to my book.

I was back at Baker Lake by 10 a.m., picked up my backpack, thanked the caretakers, and started back. On the way back I climbed to Castle Lake to take pictures of it in the sunshine., From there I cut straight over from the big flat place to the main trail. Much of the way back I worried about the flat tire I had left the day before and if I was going to have to camp by my car or if I should just change the tire and hurt my back by lifting the flat and the spare.

As I reached the trail head and opened the car door, I saw a red pickup rattling down the mining road across the canyon. I got out of the car, yelled and waved my hand to flag it down. The pickup pulled up next to me and a square-faced man in a white cowboy hat, and western shirt with shiny buttons rolled down his window. "Need a ride?" he asked.

"No, I've got a flat tire and I have a bad back, so I need help changing it."

"Glad to do it," he said. In my fatigue, the man seemed a hallucination but he and his friend changed my tire, while the driver's wife talked to me. She, too, wore a cowboy hat over her blonde hair. They owned part of a mining claim up on a ridge above Strawberry Basin, and had driven up to check their claim. Now I know they must have been Alan Getty with friends of his. Getty was a partner with Elmer Enderlin, the old miner that worked his claims at and near Fourth of July Creek from 1943 to 1995. Once my tire was changed, the red pickup followed me out to the highway and clear to Stanley. I have found that this kind of help happens a lot in Idaho. Years later I learned that Getty had once owned a garage, trailer park, and ski hill down the river from Stanley at the village of Saturday Mountain.

I had to bite my lip and play the radio loud to keep awake all the way back to Caldwell. Wayne said he had gotten along fine with the kids while I was gone. But when I asked him what he wanted to do for our anniversary the next weekend, he said, "Nothing. You spoiled it by going off by yourself and not waiting until next year when I could go, too."

I realize now I was much too obsessed with getting the book done as fast as possible. I was afraid someone else would write a guidebook before mine was finished. Yet I still remember the delicious feeling of freedom that doing the trip on my own gave me.

Little Spangle Lake

CHAPTER 13: PNEUMONIA, A LOST BOY, AND A NAIL

Donna insisted on sending the company in Colorado, Pruitt, the revised letter, a couple of photos, a sample chapter, introduction, and table of contents. There were 50 hikes by then, which I thought were plenty for a guidebook. Later I would realize 50 wasn't enough for most publishers to bother with.

In the spring of that year, 1975, I looked forward to a family pack trip even more than usual because Wayne had said we could at last go to Spangle Lakes. I needed those lakes in the center of the Sawtooths for the book. However, in early May I caught virus pneumonia and ran a fever of 102 for ten days. I stayed in bed most of that time, taking an antibiotic the doctor prescribed, thinking it would help, but it didn't.

When Memorial Day came and it was time to open the cabin I didn't feel well enough to go. It snowed three feet up there just before the weekend. Doug was the only one of our kids who wanted to go open the cabin with Wayne. The area has never had so much snow for Memorial Day since then.

One evening I got to coughing so hard I couldn't breathe and collapsed on the stairs. Wayne had heard me and came and picked me up. Luckily, his lifting my arms forced in some air and I could breathe again.

After my doctor sent me to a specialist, I found out that my coughing fit had been an asthma attack. That made me remember how when I was a child I used to get coughing fits, and my mother would get mad at me for them because she said I was coughing so hard on purpose. I used to hide in my closet so she wouldn't hear me and eat ice cubes to try to stop the coughing. The specialist prescribed codeine cough syrup and a medicine called theophylline and I began to get better.

Before the pack trip, Wayne and I, our three youngest kids, and Wayne's brother, Bruce, spent a weekend putting up paper-backed batts of pink fiberglass insulation in the cabin. Wayne, Neal, Bruce, and I stapled the insulation up with staple guns, while Hilary and Stuart measured and cut it for us. Soon we were all itching so that evening we went to what our kids called the Hot Baths. This hot spring was across the valley from our cabin, about seven miles away on a dirt road. One of our cabin neighbors owned a share in the land around the hot spring and had given us permission to use it. The hot water was mixed with cold and piped into a twelve-foot circular cattle tank. We changed into our suits in a tumbledown log shed, and then walked down to the tank.

That year the spring was overseen by bearded, pony-tailed Pegleg Mac and his shotgun. Pegleg, his wife, four children, twelve turkeys, nine geese, eight ducks and a pony lived out there in a tent, a trailer and two of the tiny log cabins from the old Alturas Lake Lodge. Our kids counted all this for us.

Pegleg walked over as we came out of the shed in our swim suits and waved a shotgun at us. "What are you doing here?" he asked.

"Mr. Hanson is our neighbor," Wayne said, draping his beach towel over his shoulders, "and he gave us permission."

"I don't mind, as long as you stay out of the spring. I had to chase a big hairy hippie out of there last week."

"We're just going to go in the tank," Wayne said.

"Did you have to shoot him?" asked Stuart, eyeing the shotgun.

"Nah. Just waved this at him and he hopped right out, ran off and left his pants."

The hot water washed away the fiberglass and the kids had fun trying to make the biggest splash. I couldn't wait for the day we would be able to shower in the cabin. It didn't seem so far off now, since the fall before Wayne and Bruce had installed a shower, sink and toilet. The toilet was connected to a septic tank so we could even use the toilet by filling its tank with water hauled 1/4 mile from Vat Creek. The creek's name came from the moonshiners' vat that had once stood beside it. Some of the logs that had enclosed the vat are still there.

In August I was well enough to go on the pack trip if I kept taking the theophylline and cough syrup. The lakes were 13 miles from the Pettit Lake and Grandjean trailheads and 18 miles from Atlanta. We went in from Pettit Lake. The trip would give me at least four new trails for the book.

Before the trip I took the kids up to the cabin for practice hikes and to see the SNRA's chief wilderness ranger, Dave Lee. He had agreed to edit my book for accuracy. After being ill for so long, I couldn't wait to get to the mountains.

Lee said he would edit my book only if I included hikes in the Boulders and on the west side of the Sawtooths. On one practice hike, we saw Dave with two rangers from the regional office in Ogden on trail bikes. When they came rumbling up, Neal, Hilary, and Stuart were lying face down on the bridge over the outlet looking for fish. After discussing fish with the kids, Lee agreed to meet with me about his corrections the next day. When he met with me, he said, "You still haven't done the Boulders or the west side of the Sawtooths. You can't use my name in the book unless you include those trails."

He wrote out a list of trails, most of which I had never heard of. They were things like the West Fork of the North Fork of the Big Wood River in the Boulders and Johnson Creek in the Sawtooths. Most of these trails had access roads that were marked on the topographic maps with a double line of dashes. That meant they were rutted and rocky and had fords instead of bridges or culverts. I agreed to do the hikes and send him the writeups to be corrected. Dave was related to Dave Williams, one of the first outfitters in the Sawtooths. Williams had guided Robert and Miriam Underhill when they made many of the first ascents in the Sawtooths in 1935. One of the whitest of White Cloud Peaks, D. O. Lee Peak was named for Dave after he died of cancer in 1981.

To begin the Spangle Lakes trip, we had Max Bitton and his son Jeff pack in our gear and food nine miles to Edna Lake. Neal, Hilary and Stuart were the kids who went with us. Doug, 19, was working at the I.D. department store in Caldwell to help with his college expenses, and Leslie, 16, was working at K-mart to earn money to be an exchange student. We didn't think anything about leaving them at our house by themselves for a week. Parents today would say we neglected them but we thought they were responsible enough to look after themselves.

From Edna Lake, we backpacked five more miles over two divides to Little Spangle Lake, where we camped. It had a wonderful view of Snowyside Peak's dinosaur back. Snowyside is the second highest mountain in the Sawtooths and has an enormous sloping snowbank on its Sawtooth Valley side.

We spent the evenings slapping mosquitoes; there were so many that they turned the blue sky gray. Our mosquito repellant, which had Deet in it rather than citronella, didn't help. Campfire smoke didn't help either so we just walked around in the evenings and then went to bed early in our bug-proof tents. I had sewed another Frostline tent for the kids, a two-person one for the three of them to squeeze into.

When some neighboring backpackers asked us if we had any mosquito stuff they could buy, we just gave them ours because it wasn't doing us any good.

In spite of the mosquitoes the kids had fun fishing with the new freeze-dry worms. We had also brought some of the new freeze dry ice cream, which the kids loved.

While at Spangle Lakes, we took two day hikes, the first was to Benedict Lake and the other was to Camp and Heart Lakes. On the way to Benedict Lake, we passed Ingeborg and Rock Slide lakes. Rock Slide Lake then had a sign Robert Jackson Lake. The Forest Service told me Robert Jackson didn't meet the requirements to have a lake named after him. In the first place he wasn't dead. He also had nothing to do with the history of the area. Between Ingeborg and Rock Slide lakes we could see to the south the two orange and black fangs of The Rakers. The route to Camp and Heart Lakes brought us right up to the dragon cliffs of Snowyside.

On our way back from Spangle Lakes we camped at Vernon Lake near Edna. The next morning, as I tried to roll our tent small enough to fit in its case, a boy about Neal's age limped toward us. He was slight with wavy brown hair and his face was wound tight with anxiety. He wore new-looking boots, and carried a backpack with a heavy, old-fashioned sleeping bag tied crooked across the top. His voice cracking, he asked, "Are you going out? Will you take me with you? I have to go to my mother's funeral."

"What did you say?" Wayne said, looking up from stuffing his sleeping bag.

Scratching the bites on his tear-streaked face, the boy explained he was on a city recreation trip from eastern Idaho to Big Spangle Lake. The other kids, including his older brother, had teased him and even thrown his tennis shoes in the fire. There was no death – he just wanted to go home, to get away from the teasing and the mosquitoes.

Forty-five minutes later as we rested under a pleated orange wall, a sturdy young man with blond good looks jogged up to us. "Oh there you are! We were so worried."

The boy scrunched down on the rock and said, "Don't make me go back to camp."

"You don't have to. We'll work something out."

Wayne arranged that the boy could stay overnight with us and a group leader would come get him in the morning and take him to the trailhead.

I thought the young man should have made the boy go back with him. I felt imposed on. The boy seemed a threat because I was afraid my kids might catch his feelings about mountains as though they were some kind of flu. Now I feel embarrassed that I wasn't more sympathetic and hospitable. Near the top of Sand Mountain Pass, the boy started limping much worse. Wayne sat him down and checked his feet. They had huge blisters. Wayne washed his feet and put band-aids and moleskin over the blisters. The boy's socks were cotton, and cotton socks often cause blisters, so Wayne gave him a pair of his own wool socks.

That evening we camped at Toxaway Lake. After dinner, I ignored the boy and took Hilary around to the other side of the lake to look at the view. There I promptly fell in a creek and had to spend the rest of the evening in my sleeping bag. The only dry clothes I had brought was a pair of shorts. That probably served me right for not wanting to help with the boy.

When we arrived back at our cabin the next afternoon, my parents, and Bruce and his two boys, Chuckie and Chad, were there. Bruce and the boys spent the night but my parents still stayed at Swiss Villa at Obsidian. In the evening a Caldwell neighbor, Betz Montgomery, arrived in her motor home with Neal's friend Robin, the son of her next door neighbor.

The next morning Wayne left to go back to work and Bruce and his boys went fishing. My parents wanted to go on a hike right away. I decided to take advantage of there being an extra car and take a hike for the book that required a car shuttle. We all drove to Iron Creek and left one car there. Then we drove in to the Stanley Lake trailhead and hiked a mile or so through the meadows to where the Alpine Way trail turns south to Iron Creek. The trail to that junction had a great view of the two triangular peaks, Mt. McGown and its neighbor, that create the classic view of Stanley Lake. At the junction my father, Hilary, Betz and I turned south toward Iron Creek.We left my mother with Neal, Stuart and Robin. My party had gone only a half mile when Betz fell while crossing a small creek and took a patch of skin off her leg. We washed and put ointment on it, but she decided to turn back and join my mother and the boys.

A day or so later my father went on a Sierra Club trip that started at Redfish. While he was gone my mother stayed at the cabin with me, Hilary, Stuart, and Hilary's friend Sarah Wallace, who had come up from Caldwell. Every day it rained a lot, so we couldn't hike or even take the kids to the beach.

One rainy morning I noticed Hilary and Sarah sitting in my parents Buick which was parked at the bottom of our driveway. While running down the hill to tell the girls to get out of the car I stepped on a nail sticking out of a board, The nail punched through the sole of my sneaker into my foot. The board with the nail was part of a sign Doug had once made that said "park here". When I sat down and tried to pull the nail out, it hurt so much I couldn't do it. As I yelled "Help, help," the girls ran to find my mother. She was on a walk around the loop road for the cabins. When she came back from her walk, she sat down on the hillside, braced her feet on a rock and pulled the nail out. "Ow!" I screamed, then looked up at my mother's anxious face, I asked her how she could bear to pull it out. She said, "I can't lift you into the car and you need to go to the clinic. You do what you have to do."

I sat in my mother's car, my foot throbbing, while she drove the 20 miles down the valley to the clinic in Stanley. Hilary, Sarah and Stuart whispered in the back seat. As she drove my mother told of the time during the Depression when her neighbor asked her mother to go into the neighbor's husband's study because she had heard a shot from in there. My grandmother did it, and found the neighbor's husband had shot himself. My mother asked my grandmother how she could bear to do this and she told her the same thing, "You do what you have to do. Your nail was easy in comparison."

At the clinic, I had a tetanus shot and got some antibiotics. The nurse practitioner, Marie Osborn, told me to soak my foot in warm water several times a day.

The next day Sarah's mother Val, six-year-old sister Liz, and Hannah, the niece of a friend of Val's, arrived to take an overnight hike with me and my kids. Even though my foot hurt I backpacked with them to Alice Lake. I didn't think Val would take the kids by herself, and I didn't want to disappoint everyone. I just soaked my foot in the creeks and lake. Marie had said warm water but I didn't think the temperature of the water really mattered.

Because it began to rain and six year old Liz was very tired we didn't go all the way to Alice Lake. Instead we camped at a pond a half mile below it. The pond is right under the skyscraper mountain called El Capitan, the one that looks as though its summit has been blown sideways. It rained so hard that night that Hilary, Sarah, and I spent much of the night mopping the tent floor with bandannas and pur shirts. Stuart stayed in Val's tent with Liz and Hannah and he dug trenches around the tent to try to keep the water out.

When we hiked out in the rain the next afternoon, we found that my father's Sierra Club trip had ended early because it had rained seven of eight days and the leader thought the planned two more days would be too miserable in so much rain. It was a good thing they came out when they did because the next day it began to snow.

The next morning my parents, Val and her girls, Hilary, Stuart and I all left for home. In the next week it snowed eight inches in the backcountry. Several parties had to be rescued.

When I got home and looked at the mail, I found Pruitt Publishing had sent me a contract, but it required me to guarantee that 2,500 copies of the book would sell in the first year. It didn't specify the printing quality, or any marketing. Wayne convinced me to turn them down. We couldn't afford to buy 2,500 copies even at wholesale with Doug in college and me only substituting. It took a while for Wayne to persuade me because I thought the book would sell well. At the time it was a huge disappointment, but actually would turn out to be a good thing.

Neal at the Queens River trailhead.

CHAPTER 14: BEARS IN THE NIGHT

The following year I wanted to start on the trails on the west side of the Sawtooths that Dave Lee had insisted on. Most of them were more than ten miles long and required several days of backpacking. I thought we could do another family trip to cover one of them, but Wayne wanted to go see the east side of the White Clouds. The kids had talked so much about them he wanted to see them, too. In addition, they had been the site of the mining controversy over mining the base of Castle Peak that got Cecil Andrus elected governor. So we planned a White Clouds trip for later that summer.

First I took Hilary and Stuart with me to visit my parents at Fallen Leaf. I wanted them to remember my grandfather's cabin and the trails there and the kids were only five and seven the last time we had been there. I had hoped that Wayne and Neal would go with us but they couldn't get away. My sister Dodie was visiting there too with her oldest son, Jimmy who was Stuart's age. With my father who was then 69, we did several short hikes and a 14-mile one from Echo Lake through Desolation Valley to Fallen Leaf. Stuart almost fell in Lake LeConte, when he peered over the edge of a slab to look for fish, but his grandpa grabbed him by a foot. It was fun for me to see some of the old familiar places again, such as the trailhead at the historic mineral spring resort of Glen Alpine. The resort had closed but the spring was still there, although its water by then had to be boiled or filtered.

When the kids and I finally got to the Sawtooth cabin that summer we worked with Wayne and Bruce on nailing paneling over the insulation we had put in the summer before. Before the White Clouds trip Wayne spent some time at the cabin hiking with us to get in shape. Only Hilary and Stuart went with us on the White Clouds trip. Doug was working at Glacier National Park in the warehouse at East Glacier, and Leslie was working on the College of Idaho paint crew in Caldwell until she left to be an exchange student in Brazil. She was going to Sao Paulo on a Rotary scholarship. Neal was trying to earn enough money for junior ski racing by having two jobs and a morning paper route. We trusted Leslie 17 and Neal 14 to manage for themselves while we were gone, though today parents wouldn't leave kids that young by themselves.

To make things easier, Wayne hired a packer from Challis named Jim Pepcorn. His horses carried our food and gear seven miles from Livingston Mill to Walker Lake. From there we day hiked to Sheep Lake and the Big Boulder Lakes and then backpacked from there to the Boulder Chain Lakes. We had to drive our pickup truck from the cabin because the engine of our GMC kept dying. Hilary and Stuart rode in the pickup shell with our packs and duffel bags.

After we hiked the seven steep miles to Walker Lake we found new snow under the trees. It was so cold by evening that Hilary and Stuart got in their sleeping bags in their tent after dinner and read. Wayne and I put on all the clothes and jackets we had brought and zipped our sleeping bags together, but we didn't get in them yet. When we went to the stream to get water for cocoa we heard a lot of clanging and hammering from above us. I hoped it wasn't bears getting into someone's food, but I had Wayne and the kids with me, so I wasn't scared.

The next day it was still cold but the sun came out and we hiked to two different places, Sheep Lake and the Big Boulder Lakes. As we started out an older man and woman came down to us from the rocks above. The woman said, "Hope we didn't scare you last night. We heard something by the creek, and thought it was a bear so we banged our pots to scare it away. Did you hear it?"

I explained that it had just been us getting water. I guess I wasn't the only one afraid of bears in the night. That morning we hiked up the creek to Sheep Lake. There, Hilary, Stuart, and Wayne fished, and I took pictures and wrote notes on the route and the lake. Hilary had started fishing again though not often. After an hour or so, I told the others it was time to leave because we needed to go see the Big Boulder Lakes. "You need to clean your fish," I told Hilary. After she had done this, Stuart came over and said, "Can I rinse them?"

Hilary handed him the stringer with four fish on it. He took it and swung it back and forth in the lake and then let go! The fish and stringer flew out and sank. Hilary screamed and started hitting Stuart in a melee of homemade blue sweaters. I took off my jeans and boots, took Hilary's pole and waded out into the lake in my underwear. After several minutes, I came up with the stringer and pulled in the fish. Only then did I notice people on the next peninsula, laughing and pointing at me.

Next we went back down the stream and up into the wildflower meadow that had the path to the Big Boulder Lakes. The path climbed scree and outcrops, passed Hook Lake and then reached the immense sapphire platters of the Big Boulder Lakes. We went on up to the highest lake, Cirque, so Wayne could catch a big fish like Neal did when we had been there before.

This lake was in splintery cream-colored rock in contrast to the white granite of the lower two lakes. It was still cold, and Hilary and Stuart didn't want to fish. They were soon bored, so I took them up above the lake to two tiny ponds in the talus, called The Kettles. They had been formed by the glacier that used to lie under the rocks until its ice stopped moving and could no longer be called a glacier. Finally, at about 5 o'clock, Wayne caught a 14 inch cutthroat and we could go back to camp.

The next day we had a big problem when we started the backpacking part of the trip. We were headed to the Boulder Chain Lakes and they were in a different drainage. To go by trail the distance was 12 miles. Jim Pepcorn had told us that we could instead go cross country from Quicksand Meadows, which were 2 miles back down the trail.

Quicksand Meadows spread out below a mountain with patches of colored rock that made it resemble a crazy quilt. Here we left the trail as directed and followed a fence around the quicksand into a forest. Once in its dim green light we searched for the gully Pepcorn said led to the pass we should cross, but we couldn't find it. Stuart pinched his lips together and didn't say anything because he had agreed not to complain if I let him take the little truck shaped rocks he'd been playing with at lunch. Hilary hadn't promised anything and kept complaining, "We're lost! Mr. Pepcorn is crazy!"

Sitting down on a log, Wayne said, "I think we're going to have to go back to the meadows and go around by the trail!"

"You stay here and I'll look for the gully," I said.

Wayne shook his head, "No, we have to stick together. We'll look for ten more minutes."

If we had to go back I wouldn't be able to add two cross country routes to the book. I didn't think ten minutes would be enough time.

Luckily we soon emerged into a steep rocky meadow next to a dry ravine. The ravine climbed to a talus-covered pass, which I realized must be Pepcorn's route. My watch already said 5:00 p.m. so I looked for a level place with some water but found neither one. We had to go on. As we climbed the ravine pikas eeked at us from the rocks and we saw them carrying little haystacks of plants that were bigger than they were. We zigzagged up the talus to keep from sliding back. Soon the surface changed to hard dirt with pebbles on it. Wayne took Hilary by the hand, and said, "Let's get out of the gully. Wait there and then bring Stuart to me." Tiptoeing over the rocks

I did that. By the time we reached the top of the pass the sun had set and ahead the two Frog Lakes gleamed silver in the twilight. It was dark before we reached the first lake and there were cow pies everywhere. We had to scrape them away before we could set up the tent. While we were scraping I heard a thrashing in the bushes and gasped. A bear! We had already had too much trouble. I yelled. but when Wayne shone his light on the moving bushes a steer appeared, tossing its head. The steer lumbered off, but my heart was thumping.

Wayne set up the stove under a willow. When the kettle boiled and I added macaroni, I knocked my elbow on the branches and the pot tipped over. I started to cry and Wayne hugged me and said, "Don't cry. We're on vacation. The grass is clean - just put the macaroni back in the pot and boil it some more." I was so exhausted that I crawled around picking up macaroni in the dark and giggling.

Pepcorn Pass as Hilary and Stuart called it wasn't the end of our difficulties on that trip. The worst was when we were crossing a snowbank above the highest Boulder Chain Lake on the trail, and boy scouts down below started yelling at Stuart. That caused him to miss his footing and fall down the snowbank 100 feet or more. Luckily he was only bruised, but Wayne swore at the scouts as loud as he could yell. No one came up to help Stuart even though they weren't far below.

In completing the hikes for the book one of the main difficulties for me was my fear of bears coming in the night. You saw that I kept worrying about bears on our White Clouds trip. I can trace that fear back to the summer I was two years old at my grandfather's cabin at Fallen Leaf Lake. One night I heard a tremendous crash and woke up screaming. My father pulled the string for the overhead light and hurried out to see what it was. My mother bent over and picked me up from the cabin crib, which was just a wooden box on legs. Above her, I saw the monster eyes of knotholes in the wall, so I hid my face against my mother's flannel nightgown as she patted my back.

My father came back inside. "Something knocked over the cooler," he said, "and broke the milk jug. It was probably a bear, but the noise scared it away."

Shivering, I listened for noises. That crash in the night is my first memory of Fallen Leaf. Because of it, my joy in mountains has always been mixed with fear. Perhaps that is one reason I find them so compelling.

The next morning my mother led me across the porch from the bunkhouse to the kitchen. We passed a lake of milk with islands of broken glass and blue and orange bits of broken dishes. The tall wooden box of the cooler lay flat on its doors.

By the time I finished breakfast, Grandma had cleaned up the porch. Next to the wash bench, Grandpa was turning the handle of a giant gray bucket that was tipped on its side. He called it a cement mixer. As he turned, it made a slurp-slurp noise. His gold-rimmed glasses perched on his nose and the sun drew little paths of gold in his reddish-blonde hair. With a shingle he scooped up a heap of gray stuff from the mixer, and carried it to a flat place behind the wash bench. Then he spread it over the ground.

Wrinkling my nose at the dusty smell, I crept close and asked, "What are you doing, Grandpa?"

"Building a new cooler," he said, smoothing the gray stuff back and forth.

"Why?" I asked.

"So we won't have any more problems with bears." He set a brown rock in the gray stuff.

"Bears?"

"A bear knocked over the cooler."

"Will the bear come back, Grandpa?" I asked, glancing up at the woods.

"No. The bear has gone far away, but if another bear comes here it can't knock over this cooler." He continued to spread the gray stuff.

"What s that?"

"Mortar. It's to stick the rocks together."

No bears ever came back to Grandpa's cabin when I was a child or teenager. More than 80 years later the stone cooler is still standing, Only after I had grown up, married, and moved to Idaho did bears begin to come again to the Fallen Leaf cabin. When they did, my cousin Pat had to replace the cabin door three times.

As I did hikes for the guidebook, my fear of bears made it hard to do the overnight and multi-day hikes I needed. I kept putting off going to any places that would take more than one day, unless I could persuade the whole family to go with me. I seldom could do that. After I persuaded the chief wilderness ranger, Dave Lee, to correct the manuscript for accuracy, I couldn't put off those long trails he insisted on any longer.

After the White Clouds trip I planned a five or six day backpacking trip up the Queens River and back down the Little Queens on the west side of the Sawtooths. Wayne had already used his vacation to take the White Clouds trip, so I would have to do the trip with Hilary and Stuart. They were then nine and eleven. and not very fast hikers. They were too young to leave at home while Wayne and Neal were at work. Doug was working in Glacier that summer, and Leslie was already in Brazil as an exchange student.

When I told Hilary and Stuart about the trip, Hilary said, "Do I have to go? We just got back, and I've already hiked a lot this summer. Can I stay here and see my friends?"

"I don't think so. I need you to go with me," I said.

Just then Neal came in and set a black and white topographic map on the table in front of me. He smelled like gasoline and his T-shirt was streaked with oil from the go-carts of the amusement park where he worked. He said, "You don't have this map, do you? Dr. Conger gave it to me for the scout trip. It's an advance sheet from the geological survey. You'll need it because it's kind of hard to find the trail. Don't you want me to go with you? I can keep you from getting lost."

I was surprised he wanted to go and said, "Wouldn't you find it boring since you've done if before?"

"I haven't had any vacation. and I haven't seen you much. I didn't get to go to the White Clouds."

I accepted his offer and Wayne said he would keep track of Hilary and Stuart so we wouldn't have to take them and could hike faster. I think Wayne kept track of those kids by taking them one at a time to the office so they wouldn't fight.

Neal and I started out by driving to the village of Atlanta. As we drove the dirt road that led from near Idaho City to the Middle Fork of the Boise River and up it, rain sounded like pebbles falling on the car. When we reached the turnoff for the side road to the Queens River trailhead, Neal looked up from his book and said, "Let's go see Atlanta. We ve never been there. Maybe if we do, the rain will stop."

Atlanta had begun as a mining town in 1864. There were still a few weathered houses, barns, and a bar or two with roofs of rusted tin. The pickups parked in front of them were rusty, too. Above the canyon gray cliffs and crumbled rocks rose to the wide point of Greylock Peak In the old log hotel, Neal played pool while I drank coffee. After an hour or so it stopped raining

We then drove back to the Queens River trailhead. Neal signed us in at the trail register and we took pictures of each other. Neal s freckles had disappeared but his dark brown hair still hung to the collar of his ski-patch-covered jacket. I wore a beige, flowered sunbonnet and octagonal wire-rimmed glasses. The grass and brush were so wet from the rain that we put on our rain chaps and wore them the rest of the day.

The first night we camped six miles up the Queens River, just past the second ford near Nanny Creek. Above the campsite, the canyon walls were a mixture of steep granite slabs and patches of fir and ponderosa pine. To my surprise I fell asleep easily. Perhaps I slept too soundly for in the morning we found an inch-wide hole in our brand-new tent. I had bought the 5-pound tent, which had a rain fly, for trips where weight was vital, so I was annoyed. Was it a bear, a squirrel, or an athletic mouse?

We continued up the Queens River for another day, then crossed two divides and descended the Little Queens River back to where it joined the Queens. Along the way we passed lakes in granite basins. The most beautiful didn't have a name and was just a royal blue pond set in a green meadow, like a sapphire in green velvet. Above the pond flitted hummingbirds feathered in red and green. Across the deep canyon of the Queens River rose the dark gray face of Mt. Everly like a giant elephant.

The second divide, High Pass, let us see North and South Raker, which resembled multi-colored knives of rock. They appeared unclimbable, but I learned that Robert and Miriam Underhill had climbed South Raker in 1935. The Underhills had brought European climbing techniques to the United States where they taught them to members of the Sierra Club such as Norman Clyde. More than 20 first ascents in the Sawtooths are credited to them.

On the fourth day, in the canyon of the Little Queens River, Neal and I reached the Scenic Lakes junction, only six miles from the trailhead. It was marked with a well-gnawed gray sign and a pile of bear scat. We had planned to camp at the junction and day hike to the lakes. After seeing the scat I wanted to climb the extra three and a half miles to the lakes to get away from the bears. I thought they wouldn't go up to the lakes because there would be less to eat.

After a mile, the trail disappeared at the base of slanting cliffs. Here a sign said "Horse travel prohibited beyond this point." Maybe the Forest Service thought a sign would keep people from trying to ride their horses up the cliffs. I wondered if we would be able to get up there on foot but Neal didn't hesitate.

After scrambling part way up the cliffs, Neal sat down on a ledge and I dropped down beside him. I was enjoying the warm sun and the glowing green of the meadow and willows below when Neal gasped. Pointing down into the willows 100 feet below us, he said "There's a bear!" Naturally, a bear would appear on this trip, just to see if I was still afraid.

Below us, a cinnamon-colored bear rustled around in the willows. Neal put on his pack and scrambled up the cliffs, with me right behind him just to be sure he would be all right. I knew he didn't like bears either because when he was only seven, he and Hilary had met a bear standing on its hind legs, sharpening its claws on a tree near our cabin, and they had run home screaming.

Above the cliffs a sketchy trail appeared and we followed it to the first of the Scenic Lakes. We set up our little orange tent at the lower end of the lake. Our campsite gave us a wonderful view of two wide, dark gray stripes of rock meeting in a V on the high cliff across the water. After supper, we explored the upper lake, where more rock stripes stuck out of the ridge like brown candles. As darkness fell, every rustle of the willows or chatter of a squirrel made the back of my neck prickle. I could smell the mud at the lake's edge. It was so cold and damp from the rain earlier in the week that we climbed into our tent before dark. When I shut my eyes, I kept seeing that afternoon's bear thrashing around in the willows.

I had dozed off when something growled outside the tent. My heart racing, I unzipped my sleeping bag and sat up. Neal woke up, raised his head and asked, "Did you hear that? Is it the bear?"

"Ssh, no, it's probably something else. I'll go out and see," I said, putting on my boots. The noise had stopped, but when I unzipped the tent door, it started up again.

I started to stand up and look out with the flashlight, but whatever it was gave a loud growl. I dove back into the tent, shaking, the blood roaring in my ears. Trembling I zipped the tent closed. Neal grabbed the flashlight and hit it on the metal canteen, but the growling continued. "Rowr, rrrr, yargh!"

Then, Neal yelled "Yee-ow-ow-ow-ow!," the war whoop he had used in the Big Horn Crags sun dance, but much louder. The growling stopped and we heard crashing as the animal plunged off through the willows down the outlet.

"Great idea, Neal," I said, patting his shoulder. The starlight from outside was so faint it showed Neal only as the silhouette of a sleeping bag with hair.

"Now we'll never know if it was the bear or not."

"Maybe it left footprints in the mud. Are you going to be able to go back to sleep?"

"Not for a while," he said. "Maybe I could tell you the story of the book I've been reading."

I wished I had a giant flashlight with lots of batteries. I'd leave it on the rest of the night, but all we had was a pen light and it's batteries were nearly run down. After a few minutes of telling the story of *The Two Towers*, from Tolkien's trilogy, *Lord of the Rings,* Neal s voice trailed off. I lay awake, listening for footsteps the rest of the night. I counted sheep, I counted mountains, I counted kinds of flowers but I stayed on edge. How could he sleep with a bear outside somewhere? I wanted someone to stay awake with me or to keep watch while I slept, but I didn't dare wake Neal up. He needed his sleep for the energy to carry his pack out the next day. I also didn't want him to know how scared I felt. I had read that parents must always act strong and competent or else they'll make their kids fall apart. Then I heard growling again. Frozen, I listened for footsteps. There weren't any, and then I realized it was just Neal snoring.

When I looked for tracks in the mud on the lake shore the next morning there weren't any. The mud had frozen and a skin of ice coated the edge of the water.

All the way down to the river that morning, Neal beat on our smallest cooking pot with a rock, smiling a funny little smile. By the time he stuffed the pot in his pack when we ate lunch at the river, its bottom was concave. "Why did you do that? You ruined our pot!" I said.

"Well, you can pound it out again, can't you? It worked. You didn't see any more bears, did you?" he said, laughing.

He could joke about it, but as I glanced at the tooth marks on the Scenic Lakes sign I couldn't laugh. Yet, I realized that if I could stay in a tent where something growled outside and not run off screaming, I could manage my bear phobia. I would still be afraid, but I could handle it well enough to finish writing my guide book.

As we hiked down the Little Queens River toward the trailhead, I thought about the explorers and homesteaders. They must have feared the dark, bears, and the unknown, the way I did. However, very few if any admit it in their writings. The closest I found to admitting fear is Isabella Bird in *A Lady's Life In the Rocky Mountains*, which was first published in 1879. After an encounter with a bear near Lake Tahoe one afternoon that scared her horse so much it ran away without her she wrote, "I found an irregular wooden inn, with a lumber-wagon at the door, on which was the carcass of a large grizzly bear, shot behind the house this morning. I had intended to ride ten miles farther, but, finding that the trail in some places was a blind one, and being bewitched by the beauty and serenity of Tahoe, I have remained here…"

Yet, as I thought back to how I had felt at the beginning of the trip, I realized again that part of the attraction of mountain journeys is thinking about what might happen, with the prickling of fear going up and down your spine.

Book cover of the first edition.

CHAPTER 15: HIKING LIKE CRAZY TO FINISH THE BOOK

I still remember how I hiked like crazy to finish my guide book in the summer of 1977. I had finally found a publisher, Signpost Books in Edmonds, Washington, and had only that summer to do all the rest of the hikes for the book. I felt I must do all the hikes the chief wilderness ranger, Dave Lee, insisted I include. He was afraid a guidebook would cause overuse of the trails on the east side of the Sawtooths that were easy to reach. The trails he wanted me to put in started near Grandjean, Graham, and Atlanta on the west side of the Sawtooths, and near the North Fork of the Big Wood River in the Boulder Mountains above Ketchum. These hikes added up to about 170 miles. Louise Marshall, head of Signpost, the publisher I had found, wanted the manuscript by December 1st.

Wayne tried to caution me about dealing with Signpost. He asked, "Did they send you a contract?"

Of course they hadn't, but I still believed they were going to publish the book. I remember how excited I was. Book sales would fulfill Wayne's request that I earn the money to finish the cabin. The cabin had been partly finished since he had made the request, but I still wanted it completed. I had no idea then how little money writers make. I thought the book would mean I wouldn't need to keep substituting and looking for a teaching job.

Shortly after Signpost said they'd publish my book I received a letter from a man named Luther Linkhart. He said he had a contract from Wilderness Press to write a guidebook to the Sawtooth National Recreation Area and wondered if I'd help him. Wilderness Press was one of the publishers Donna had written for me when she had sent out all the letters and they had rejected my book. They hadn't even wanted to look at the manuscript. So I was annoyed at Linkhart's letter, feeling that he had stolen my idea. Besides I already had an oral agreement with Signpost, so I told him no.

I didn't know if I could get all the trails hiked that summer. My kids ranged in age from 10 to 21 and I would have to take Hilary and Stuart with me. They couldn't be left on their own when Wayne was at work. Wayne had already asked me not to be gone as much as I had the summer before because he found it hard to keep track of the kids left home and to keep up with the housework. The teens at home were supposed to help him but evidently didn't.

My fear had worsened from hearing the animal growl outside the tent on the Queens River trip. Several of the roads to the trailheads for these hikes were double dashed on the topographic maps. That meant big rocks and no bridges or culverts.

I also worried that too much hiking would destroy my kids' liking for it. I still wanted to hand down to them the love of hiking I had received from my parents. When I remember how seriously I took getting all the hikes on Lee's list done that one summer I have to laugh. Louise at Signpost had not told me how many hikes I had to have or that a ranger needed to edit the manuscript.

It was lucky that we'd had very little snow that winter. It had limited our skiing, but it allowed me to start hiking much earlier than usual. In late June, three of my children, Doug, Hilary, and Stuart accompanied me on a trip to cover three of Lee's trails on the west side of the Sawtooths. I hadn't expected Doug to go, but he was doing an internship at Wayne's office for college credit and hadn't started it yet. Neal stayed home with Wayne because he was taking driver training and running go-carts again, and still had his morning paper route.

This hike began at the old mining town of Atlanta. Getting there meant 41 miles of dirt road along the North and Middle Forks of the Boise River. Above the old buildings of Atlanta modern log houses hid in the trees. Across the canyon ledges sloped up to the bare summit of Greylock Peak. It may have been named by Chinese miners who couldn't pronounce Gray Rock, or by other miners making fun of the Chinese.

From the main campground, Powerplant, our plan was to backpack up the Middle Fork of the Boise eight miles and then take side trails to Timpa and Leggit lakes. By the time we reached the trailhead and started out, it was at least 85 degrees. After two or three miles, I was so hot I felt I needed a salt tablet to keep from fainting. My dad had raised me to think that salt tablets were essential on hikes. I took one from my pocket and put it on my tongue, but it just made me thirstier, Today, experts believe hikers get plenty of salt from food, and salt tablets don't help.

Just then Stuart said "Can't we stop and rest? I m hot."

Doug said, "We need to keep going. You remember Warty, the wart hog?"

"Yes," said Hilary. "You told us about him in the Big Horn Crags."

"Remember how he was trying to sell the ski binding he invented out of a mousetrap? One day he hitched a ride to Jackson with his binding..." Doug launched into a new Warty story and Stuart walked right along without complaining.

After eight hot miles of hiking we reached our planned campsite at the confluence of the river with Rock Creek. On a flat beside alders, we set up our tents. Above us rose cliffs and rock faces. Hilary and Stuart used the little green Frostline tent I had sewed for the Spangle Lakes trip. It weighed only three pounds with its poles. My tent was the larger Frostline one for two people, and Doug had a dome tent he had bought. By then we had begun to use a butane stove, so there was no need to gather firewood. The kids spent the evening fishing and reading. I sat under the alders beside the river writing up my notes and listening to the splashing of the high runoff. In the evening we took turns reading aloud from *The Hobbit*.

About midnight, I heard footsteps and breaking branches. I thought it was a bear or a cougar. When the steps came closer, I screamed.

"What's wrong, Mom?" Doug called out.

"Something's out there," I said.

"I didn't hear anything. Did you look out?"

When I unzipped the tent, I saw four deer silhouetted in the moonlight and felt foolish.

"It's just some deer."

"That's usually what you hear in the night. It was stupid to scream. I might have run over to see what was the matter and broke my leg."

“I’m sorry,” I sighed. How could I be so stupid?

To go to Timpa Lake the next morning, we first had to ford the river. It was knee high whitewater, but by leaving our boots on and again using branches for poles we made it across. In a quarter mile we had to cross Rock Creek, also through whitewater. After 2 miles, the trail crossed back over Rock Creek. Here the creek was wider and calmer. Many logs had fallen in an intricate mat. The kids walked across, stepping over each log, but I was too afraid I’d fall in to stand up. I crawled across, and in one place used my knife to cut off a branch that stuck up in my way.

Timpa Lake was remarkable only for its clouds of mosquitoes, but it was pretty with grass-lined shores and a cliff-covered bluff. There were so many mosquitoes I put on my rain poncho and chaps, and mosquito headnet to eat lunch. It was hard to eat because to take a bite I had to raise up the front of the headnet.

When we got back to camp, we packed up and took our stuff back down four miles to where Mattingly Creek entered the river and camped beside it.

The next morning we backpacked down the river a mile, put our packs in green garbage bags and hid them in the brush. Then we started climbing the side trail to Leggit Lake. There wasn’t any sign and it started out as a jeep trail so I wasn’t sure we were going the right way. It was so hot that Doug asked to borrow my sunbonnet because he had forgotten a hat. He said, “Don’t you dare take a picture.” I took one anyway. After only five minutes he took the sunbonnet off and tied a bandanna around his head. He was too hot to tell the kids any more of Warty’s adventures. Instead, Hilary told her own stories to keep herself and Stuart going.

After a mile or so the jeep trail turned off to the east up the side of the canyon at a campsite. From the campsite, a path forded Leggit Creek to its west side, and then faded out. The topographic map showed that this path was the correct trail, so we crossed the creek and went up alongside it. Soon a path reappeared and we passed a thousand-foot black cliff. It was too close to noon for it to shade us. Before long the path disappeared again. I insisted we keep going, but the kids muttered about mean mothers. Stuart said, “We’ve already gone far enough for you to write this up. Why can’t we go back now?”

“I can’t write what the lake looks like without seeing it.”

It took us until 1:30 to reach the lake. When we did, the one shady campsite was occupied by two people in their sleeping bags. I started to lead the kids around the lake in the opposite direction. “Why can’t we go over there?” asked Stuart. “Ssh, come on,” I said, my face feeling hot, “don’t bother them.”

The lake was surrounded by mountains and towers that were so short it seemed as though we had reached a lake in the sky. None of the kids caught any fish that afternoon, and we didn’t get back to Atlanta with our packs until 6:30. It took us until after midnight to reach the cabin, even with Doug driving part of the way.

The next morning, I turned on the power and the switch to the hot water heater. The water heater sat next to the sink in the corner of the great room. We had had a well drilled the autumn before and had turned on the water for the first time on Memorial Day weekend. As soon as the water was hot, we took our first showers in the cabin. Before this we had to go 18 miles to the pay showers at Redfish or 12 miles to the hot springs the kids called the Hot Baths.

As I watched the water droplets in the shower that morning, I remembered the water diamonds in the spray of the outdoor shower at my grandfather's cabin at Fallen Leaf. The light in our cabin's bathroom wasn't bright enough to make diamonds in the spray but after eight summers with no showers at our cabin the drops seemed like diamonds.

Later that day I started a load of wash in the old washing machine we had saved for 13 years for the cabin. When I noticed Stuart opening the lid and his light brown curly hair hanging over the machine, I said, "Don't add any more clothes. If you overload it, the washer won't last very long."

"I'm not putting anything in. I'm just watching the clothes go round. It seems like a miracle that we can wash clothes in the cabin." It did to me, too.

A few days later it was Fourth of July weekend. The whole family except Leslie, who was still in Brazil, made a loop trip from Grandjean, a small hot springs resort on the west side of the Sawtooths. We would cover two more of the long trails that I needed for the book, trails that led to Baron, and Elk lakes from Grandjean. I had thought the loop from Grandjean to Baron Lakes, over Baron and Cramer Divides and down the South Fork of the Payette past Elk Lake was only 38 miles. It was raining hard when we came to a junction with the South Fork of the Payette trail on the west side of Cramer Divide. Here a sign said "Grandjean 18". I thought the sign should say 12 and that it was only a mile more to Elk Lake where we planned to camp. We had already hiked six miles that morning in the rain. It had rained the first two days of the trip as well.

"Grandjean 18?" Wayne asked, looking at the sign. "What? It's supposed to say 12. Let me see the map."

The rain had fogged up Wayne's glasses and water dripped off his cowboy hat. Granite towers on the canyon walls appeared and disappeared in the mist as though they were moving. In such dim light, our bright red and blue ponchos seemed to glow.

Doug came over to look at the map, his hair so wet it hung in brown strings. "I thought you said it was only a mile to Elk Lake from this junction. Where's the next map, Edaho Mountain?"

I looked at the three maps I had covered with clear adhesive shelf paper. It was hard to read them because it was raining so hard it sounded like frying bacon. The border of the map I held did say Edaho Mountain for the next map, but I only had Mt. Cramer, Warbonnet, and Grandjean. "I don't have that one," I said, thinking how could I be so stupid as to not notice what the Warbonnet map said on its edge.

"How could you leave out a whole map? I thought we were hiking with an expert," Wayne said, laughing.

It kept on raining and three miles from the junction we had to cross a side creek, Benedict Creek, on a foot log. One of Hilary's feet slipped on the wet log and she fell, with that foot trapped between the foot log and another log. She screamed and I thought she'd broken her leg. She was stuck there but Wayne and Doug managed to pull her out and lay her down on the river bank. Luckily, her leg was only bruised, and after resting a half hour she was able to go on the three more miles to camp at Elk Lake. The next day she didn't have any trouble hiking the 12 more miles to the end of the trail at Grandjean. In fact she stomped in the puddles as the other kids did.

I wished Idaho weather weren't so changeable. At Fallen Leaf it would have been 75 degrees with no rain. Luckily, the four days of our trip were the only time it rained that whole summer. Wayne said we should have hired ourselves out to end the drought.

We were very glad to welcome our daughter Leslie back from Brazil on July 20. The next week she was to start her summer job with the College of Idaho paint crew. The first thing she wanted to do was go to the mountains and go on a hike. She said it had to be new and very beautiful. "I haven't seen any real mountains for a year."

So we went to an unnamed off-trail lake right under Thompson Peak, the highest mountain in the Sawtooths. Dave Lee had told me not to put that lake in the book because it was too hard a hike for most people. He called it Thompson Cirque Lake, but some locals now call it Profile Lake. It is the second lake by that name in the Sawtooths. When we reached the trailhead at Redfish, Neal and Stuart didn't want to go. They just wanted to stay at Redfish and fish. So we left them there.

We took the trail to Marshall Lake and then turned off it to a pretty pond. From it we hiked up a long, steep slope that was mostly talus. Halfway up it were ledges with big pines. After we rested there, Wayne said he was just going to stay there because it was so hot. Doug, Hilary, Leslie and I made it to the lake all right after a tedious climb. It had pretty blue water but all its shores were rock with no plants or trees or flowers. At least Leslie thought it was beautiful.

Back at Redfish Neal and Stuart held up the string of fish they had caught and we admired them. Then I saw a sign by the creek, "Closed to fishing."

"Where did you catch these fish?"

"In the creek," Stuart said.

"Didn't you see this sign?"

The boys both shook their heads, but they must have seen it. We quickly put the fish in the car. There wasn't a Fish and Game officer there to scold the boys so we had to do it ourselves.

After resting a couple days at home, there were only 12 days left before the kids had to register for school. I still had several trails to cover. There were four hikes in the Boulder Mountains, two in the White Clouds, and three in the Sawtooths.

I planned to take Hilary, and Stuart to the cabin with me to see how many I could get done. As we were packing the evening before, Neal decided to go with us. To do this he had to get a substitute for his paper route and get time off from running the go-carts.

To get ahead on the hikes, we took one hike as a side trip on the drive to the cabin. From Stanley we drove east along the Salmon River and then south up Rough Creek into the White Clouds. At the trailhead, the kids rummaged through the luggage to find their day packs, jackets, and fishing stuff. They were ready to start out before I was, so I let them go ahead.

I put on my back brace as usual, tied my sweater around my waist, buckled on a fanny pack containing my camera and film, and on top of it put a knapsack with water and lunches. Clutching my notebook, pen, and a topographic map in one hand, I started out. The trail led up the wooded canyon of Rough Creek with no view of high peaks. The kids stopped and then waited for me. At the canyon's head, we turned off the trail and descended a half mile on a faint path to the lake.

It was just a little green pond in wooded hills, but all around it grew banks of pink and yellow monkey flowers. So many fish were jumping they looked and sounded like popcorn. When I reached the shore, Stuart was looking all around, turning out his pack and Neal's. The lures on his dirty yellow hat jingled. "You made us be in such a hurry we left all the fishing poles in the car."

"Who was in such a hurry? You and Neal didn't want to wait."

Neal cut willow poles and taped the reels onto them. The tape didn't stay on well and only two fish were caught, but at least the kids got to try to catch the jumping fish.

That evening at the cabin I fixed sandwiches for the next day's hike on the table that was covered with orange oilcloth. Stuart frowned and said, "Sandwiches? Are we going on another hike? Can't we have a rest day?"

"Yes, we're going on another hike. Before school starts I have to hike all the trails Dave said I needed to do if I want him to correct the book."

Neal had looked at my list of hikes and planned out the order to take them in, but Stuart had not thought about how tired he'd be if we followed that schedule. If Stuart needed a rest day maybe I could alternate which kids I took with me. To get all the hikes done by the time school started I had to hike every day but the kids didn't. They were old enough to stay by themselves some of the time.

So I asked Neal to stay with Stuart the next day, and Hilary to hike with me. Neal wanted to go to Sun Valley, so I drove him, Stuart, and our dog, Trixie, there before Hilary and I started hiking. On Hilary's next rest day, she stayed at the cabin and read, washed the dishes, painted pictures of the mountains, and practiced her violin. The next time it was Hilary's turn to hike Neal said, "Can I just drive to Sun Valley? It would save time. I'll take you and Hilary to the hike on the way."

"What are you going to do there?"

"Rent bikes and ice skates, eat ice cream. I'll come back and get you whenever you say."

So the next day, Neal, looking too short to be old enough to drive, drove Hilary and me to a trailhead in the Boulder Mountains on the way to Sun Valley. That day Hilary and I climbed 3,000 feet to the West Pass Creek Divide, where some of the mountains are red and covered with cliffs. I didn't take Hilary to Sun Valley on the days I hiked with the boys because I didn't think it was safe for her to be there alone. I didn't think about the lack of safety at the cabin, where we had no phone. The cabin's remoteness protected it from nefarious people, but not from household accidents. I refused to worry and thought Hilary, then 12, was old enough to deal with most problems.

After three hikes in three days I came down with a cold. I couldn't afford to take any time off, so as my rest day, I drove the children around to a campground near the Graham guard station on the west side of the Sawtooths. An Idaho City ranger had warned me that the 28-mile long access road was a typical "Idaho freeway." When I asked him if that meant it was good for a dirt road he said no, he meant the opposite. The road was so bad I was sure the only time any work had been done on it since it was built as a wagon road in 1887 was when a Civilian Conservation Corps crew widened it in the 1930s.

Soon after we turned onto the road to Graham, something under the hood of our Suburban began to rattle. Then the radiator started boiling. Oh no – car trouble could strand us for days. It was a bad place to be stuck for there was very little traffic. Stopping on top of a rise to see what was the matter, I said, "Stay in the car unless it starts rolling. If it does, jump out."

"I'll help you Mom," said Neal.

"No, please stay in the car. If I need you, I'll ask."

I was afraid Hilary or Stuart would fall down the steep hillside below the road. When I raised the hood I found the air filter had come loose. Screwing it back on stopped the boiling only until the filter bounced off again at the next patch of rocks. Finally, I tied the filter on with nylon cord. The dust from the dirt road made my cold worse.

When we reached the high point of the road, granite splinters and towers spread out before us. It reminded me of what I had read in Carrie Adell Strahorn's 1915 book, *Fifteen Thousand Miles by Stage*. She described the Sawtooths as "the grandest art view in the state." I would have appreciated the art view a lot more if the road had been better.

On the way down from the summit, a few of the switchback corners were so sharp I had to back up to get around. I kept thinking about the father of one of the girls in Leslie's Brownie troop. He had died when his jeep rolled off the Graham road. I kept shivering. The road was one of the most hair raising I had ever been on. It led past a side road to the trailhead we would start from and then went down through forest. A campground was just before a bridge over the North Fork of the Boise. From it the road led to the guard station. The bridge washed away several years later and to reach the guard station now you have to drive through the river. We set up our tents and the kids fished in the river and played kickball. Neal visited with a couple camping with their ten-month-old twin boys. The young man wired our air filter on so it wouldn't come loose again. His mending job lasted until after we finished all that summer's hikes. That night my nose stuffed up so much it felt as though someone had poured glue into it and I slept very little.

The next morning my nose started draining so I felt a little better. We drove three miles back up the road to the main trailhead. Here one trail went up the North Fork of the Boise and over a divide to the South Fork of the Payette. The other went up a creek called Bayhouse and over a divide to Johnson Creek and up it to Pats Lake. We took that one and soon met a flock of sheep that raised such a cloud of dust I dampened my sunbonnet with my water bottle and tied it over my nose. The sheepherder, who didn't speak English, tried to give Neal one of the new puppies his dog had. By using gestures to create several dogs in the air, Neal convinced him we already had enough dogs. After six miles or so the trail reached meadows with a view of peaks ahead. Here we ran out of water and found Johnson Creek was dry. It was too hot a day to go on without water, so we turned back, hiked out and drove back to the cabin. We ate supper at a restaurant in Stanley. In my journal I wrote, "Very tired but relieved to be off that hairy road."

After the Graham trip I let the kids have a rest day with paddle boats and kayaks at Redfish. The day after that Hilary and I hiked from the ford of Alpine Creek six miles up Alturas Creek to the summit above its headwaters, which is called Mattingly Creek Divide. If I could have driven through the ford of Alpine Creek I could have driven two miles farther but without four wheel drive I didn't dare try.

After two more hikes, alternating kids as before, my friend Lorry Roberts came to the cabin to hike with us and take pictures for my book. She was head of graphic arts at the J.R. Simplot potato company in Caldwell. I had saved the jeep trail to Washington Basin in the White Clouds for her hike because the close together contour lines on the topographic map meant cliffs. I thought that meant it would be spectacular. Dave Lee hadn't mentioned it, probably because it had a jeep road, not a pack trail. The road to the trailhead ran through a deep ford about 1/4 mile before it turned into a jeep trail and I parked before the ford. Stuart got out and measured the depth of the water with a stick to show me it was only eight inches deep. I still refused to drive through it because a quarter mile of extra walking was a lot better than getting stuck. When we reached the jeep trail, it was full of football-sized rocks.

Neal and Stuart had both brought books to read as they hiked, but Hilary walked with Lorry and talked to her. I didn't see how the boys could walk the rocky jeep track while reading without tripping but they did. The track led over a ridge with a view of the distant white and orange-gray face of Castle Peak. After we went down to another ford and crossed it, the jeep trail steepened and became rockier. Stuart finished his book, scowled at Neal and said, "May I please have that book back that I loaned you?"

Neal clutched the book. "I'm not finished."

"I want it back now!" Stuart picked up small rocks and started throwing them at Neal's legs. At this, Neal picked up a rock the size of his fist, raised his arm, and swung it back and forth.

I grabbed Neal, took the rock and the book and yelled,

"Stop this right now. Sit there and be quiet." I was embarrassed the boys were fighting in front of Lorry. Since Neal had just gotten his driver's license. I thought at age 16 he was much too old to fight with his brother.

Neal sat down and leaned back against the steep hillside. Stuart stood frowning until I pushed on his shoulders, and sat him down in the middle of the road. Then I lectured both boys about rock throwing and trying to get along. When I caught up with Lorry, I said "I was afraid you would think I was a terrible mother." She just said, "It's been so long since my girls were that age I can't remember how they acted." She had three daughters who were then in their twenties.

When we reached Washington Basin, it was more beautiful than I had figured, The cliffs of the surrounding peaks were all striped or patched with red, white and gold, but their details were blurred from the smoke of California forest fires. Mine tunnels and a few old log cabins and cabin ruins stood in the basin. In it was a dried-up pond with scattered timbers and a rusty boiler on the far side. Because of the smoke, Lorry couldn't get any good pictures for the book but she tried.

I later learned that one of the old cabins had belonged to George Washington Blackmon, an African-American who lived and mined in the basin around 1900. Blackmon is in a photograph of the carpenters who built Redfish Lake Lodge in 1929.

After Lorry left the following evening, we packed up and got ready to go home the next day. Taking our last hike on the way home instead of doing it from the cabin saved a whole day and we had to be home in time for the kids to register for school. As I drove to the trailhead north of Stanley, Neal and Stuart got into another argument. When we got to the trailhead above Stanley Lake, Neal said, "I'm just going to stay at the car and read and ride my bicycle. It will make it easier for you if I don't go."

Without Neal, things still didn't go smoothly. After a mile and a half the trail disappeared in Elk Meadows. We had to wade bogs and the creek and detour around three bulls before we found the trail again. I flapped my red poncho to scare the bulls away while we walked past them. I didn't know that waving things at bulls just aggravates them. Luckily the bulls didn't charge the poncho.

Beyond the meadow the trail to the lake turned off up the canyon wall to Elizabeth Lake. Stuart stopped and frowned at me and said, "This isn't the right way. Can't you tell? The trail goes on up the creek. Another wild goose chase!"

"This is the right way even if the trail is faint," I said, showing him the map.

Stuart studied it, then said, "It wouldn't seem so bad if I still had something to read, but I finished my book."

"Here, I'll lend you my other book," Hilary said, slipping off her pack. "That will help. It's a Ramona book and you'll love it."

She unzipped her pack, gave the book to Stuart and we began to climb, both children reading as they walked.

When we reached the lake, I took pictures and wrote up my notes on the hike. It was just a lake set in wooded ridges with a cliff on a small peak above, but it was still pretty. A log floated near the edge with a row of tiny firs on it. Hilary and Stuart just sat down and kept on reading. They had brought their fishing poles but didn't get them out. I realized they were thoroughly tired of hiking.

In the meadows on the way back, Stuart stumbled and dropped Hilary's book into a fresh cow pie. When he picked the book up, it dripped green slime.

"Stuart, you lump head. That's a library book, and I'll have to pay for it," Hilary roared, raising her fist.

I wiped the book off with a bandanna, but the pages had turned greenish brown. I tried using water but all it did was wrinkle them.

Hilary snatched the book. "You'll have to pay for the book. It's ruined."

Trying to calm them down, I said, "In the story Ramona wrote on the library book so she could keep it. Maybe you were trying to keep this book, Stuart?"

Hilary and Stuart both laughed, their tanned and dirty faces looking happier than they had all day. Back in Caldwell the next week I figured how many miles they had hiked that summer. It was over 150 apiece.

That made me realize my finishing the hikes for the book had been an emotional challenge for the whole family. I wondered how John Muir's wife and daughters had felt when he went off to the mountains for months at a time. At least Muir hadn't had to take his daughters with him.

Publisher Cliff Cameron.

I had completed all the hikes Dave Lee had wanted me to do, so I called Louise Marshall to ask when Signpost planned to send me a contract for the book. She wasn't there but her assistant, Cliff Cameron, said they'd send onelater that fall. He said Louise wanted to see the completed manuscript and the maps and photos first.

One afternoon after Doug and Leslie left for college in mid-September, I came home from doing errands and found Hilary and Stuart marching around in the yard. They carried signs that they had drawn with markers on the backs of old Andrus posters. The signs said, "Parents Unfair. " When I asked why they were doing this, Hilary said, "You won't let me move my room to the basement even though Doug's not there any more."

Stuart said, "You said I had to do my homework before dinner. It's MY homework and I can do it when I want to, and I want to do it LATER!"

I was embarrassed. What would the neighbors think? By the time I got the kids calmed down and indoors, it was time to cook dinner. They liked to get trophies for their ski races, so I thought it might help their attitudes if I gave them trophies for hiking. So I ordered a trophy engraved with the miles for Stuart and a silver-plated candy dish engraved with the miles for Hilary. I don't know if it helped or not, but it made me feel less guilty about having made them hike so much. Hilary still wanted to move to the basement and Stuart still wanted to do his homework at bedtime. When I asked Neal about getting him a trophy he said he already had plenty of them and he'd rather have a check toward his ski racing.

That fall, when I wasn't substitute teaching, I worked on the book, trying to get it done by Signpost's December 1st deadline. I still used the manual typewriter Wayne had in college, which had the elite type that was hard to read. I edited and rewrote the manuscript and drew new maps on poster board with a calligraphic fountain pen. I used India ink, which was blacker than calligraphic ink, but tended to clog the pen. Getting the hike descriptions clear and accurate was so difficult it would have been easier to describe fictional ones. So much typing made my shoulders feel like clenched fists.

Signpost at last sent me a contract, in November, and after consulting with Wayne I signed it. Louise's daughter Ann sent me the edited manuscript suggesting changes, and Dave Lee sent me his copy of the manuscript with corrections. I was still working on the book until a few days before Christmas. When I sent the manuscript, maps and photos to Louise and called to see if they had arrived, she told me the book would be out in the spring. I could hardly wait. It was five years since I had started writing it.

After I made the suggested changes and returned the manuscript, I didn't hear anything for three months. In April Louise sent me a notice that she had sold the company to her assistant, Cliff Cameron. When I called him to see how my book was progressing, he said, "We still plan to publish the book this spring. It shouldn't be a problem."

By the time we went to the cabin in July of 1978, I hadn't heard anything from Cliff. Was the company still in business?

I was afraid the kids wouldn't want to hike because of my over-hiking them the year before but they did. Hilary and Stuart thought of places they wanted to go like Upper Redfish Lakes and Observation Peak and I took them there. At Upper Redfish their interest was in catching frogs rather than going to the upper lake, Lake Kathryn, with me. On Observation Peak, they were much more interested in going to see what was left of the Greenback Mine below it than they were in the amazing view of all the mountains. Neal couldn't go with us because his summer job running the go-carts had become more demanding and he still had his morning paper route. He was able to take time off only to go with us on a backpacking trip in the Wind Rivers in Wyoming. Because of my book writing it was the first time we hiked outside of Idaho other than at Fallen Leaf. (Although Wayne and I had hiked in the Tetons on our honeymoon.)

In November 1978, a year from when I signed the contract, Cliff called and told me he had been working on five books at once and would get mine to the printers in two weeks. However, it was January before I received the galley proofs and in February the page proofs. Cliff told me they had found a major error in the book just before they were due to send it to the printer. The road running from Hailey and Ketchum north to Stanley and east to Challis wasn't US Highway 93 any more. It had been changed to Idaho 75. Cliff said he and his wife Mary Ann had stayed up all one night to fix it everywhere in the text and on the maps.

When I visited Cliff and Mary Ann in Edmonds, Washington, a year or so later I found that their company was so small their typesetting machine lived in their laundry room with their washer and dryer and a giant box of laundry detergent. The typesetter was the kind of machine that made type from holes in paper tape. Computers had not yet become common in publishing.

On my March birthday, a year from when Cliff had bought the company, a padded mailing envelope arrived with the first copy of my book. It was a little blue paperback only three-eighths of an inch thick. It had white lettering and a half-page photograph of Fishhook Creek Meadow below saw-toothed mountains on the cover. The sky was turquoise and the trees a little too green, but there was my name right below the title.

To my dismay, some of the photos inside of the book had the tops of the mountains cut off. For me it was as though they had cut off people's heads. Cliff had used a local printer and evidently they didn't know any better. I imagined Cecil Andrus, then Secretary of the Interior, who had written the foreword, was embarrassed by the poor printing. At least the book was done, and people could use it. Amid my happiness, I still worried that by over-hiking the kids I had killed the family tradition I was so eager to pass on.

Five days later I received a whole box of books and started selling them. Now no family who bought my book would drive the Fourth of July Creek or Hell Roaring roads without knowing how bad they were. Hikers would know that some trails disappeared part way along and how to find them again. They would be able to find the routes that had no signs or were secret unofficial trails like the path to Saddleback Lakes under the Elephant's Perch.

Doug wrote from college in Salt Lake City, *"I just received a copy of your book. It's just beautiful. I'm really happy for you. After all these years it's finally a reality. The experience must be rewarding, kind of like building a bridge, and now people can drive across it and admire the landscape."*

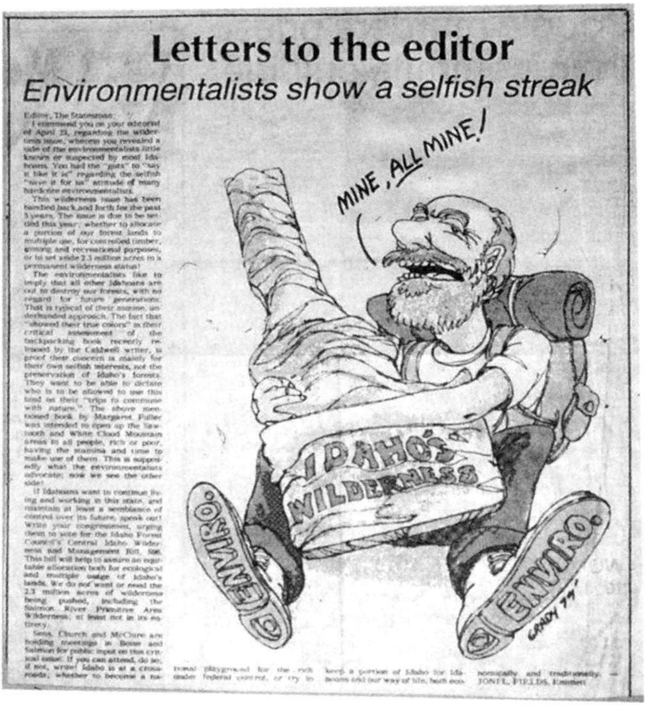

Letters to the editor

Environmentalists show a selfish streak

Cartoon in the *Idaho Statesman*.

CHAPTER 16: SLIDE SHOWS AND A CARTOON

Cliff had printed black and white brochures on newsprint about my book and I sent them to bookstores and sporting goods stores. After receiving a brochure, Lou Florence, who owned Sawtooth Mountaineering in Boise, called and offered to help with book publicity if I would give a slide show at his store. Lou had worked for an advertising agency in New York City so his story for the *Idaho Statesman*, the Boise newspaper, emphasized controversy. It said some people questioned whether a book that gave away secret places to hike should have been published. In New York he had learned that controversy got people's attention and the controversy he used for my book was that it gave away secret places.

I had included my secret routes that weren't on any maps. They led to some of the most beautiful places in the state, such as Castle Lake in the White Clouds and Saddleback and Goat lakes in the Sawtooths. When I had first learned about these places and tried to get directions without success, I felt shut out. I thought people had a right to know how to reach these beautiful places. You shouldn't have to live in an Idaho town for four generations first. That is why I included more than a dozen secret places. For some of these I had just taken a topographic map (if there was one) and followed the terrain. As I hiked to a secret place I often found a path, sometimes only on the way back.

After Lou's story appeared, people wrote letters to the editor for and against my book. John Accola in an article in the *Statesman* quoted Lou as saying, "I think it's the definitive book on the Sawtooths, a real boon to any backpacker or climber." The paper published an editorial cartoon of a burly backpacker hugging the state of Idaho with the word wilderness on it. The editorial with it said, *"These are some of the same folks who argue in favor of preserving wilderness for the people. We always thought they meant all the people....Here they are, whining and fuming over a publication that would allow more people to enjoy wilderness."*

A few readers even wrote to me personally to object to it. I didn't see why they thought a guidebook was such a bad thing if it kept families from disastrous hikes and from getting stuck on bad roads. I regarded the book as a way to keep hikers safe as well as happy with their adventures. No ranger should tell a person who inquires to just climb up the waterfall when there is a path.

Opponents thought the book would bring too many people to Idaho's backcountry.

If you don't entice people out into the wild places by describing how beautiful they are and telling how to reach them, people won't care about them. Then no one will contact their Congressman or woman about threats to it.

When I gave the slide show at Lou's store, so many people (maybe 70) came they didn't all fit in the small basement room. A few extra squeezed in by sitting on the floor and others by lying down with their legs under the screen. Still others sat on the stairs even though they couldn't see the screen. I felt anxious with so many people there. I had shown only a dozen slides, when the first plastic slide cube stuck in the Bell & Howell projector. It was a new projector Wayne had given me for Christmas. As soon as Lou found the light switch, I worked on getting the slides unstuck. As I worked, people started shouting out questions. It was hard to answer questions while working on the projector. Then Lou called out for everyone to save their questions until after the show.

After freeing the slide cube, I continued the show, but the slides stuck several more times. When I had signed several books and was packing up the projector, Lou said the best additional publicity for my book would be more slide shows. "First, you need a slide show lesson. Call me next week and we'll arrange it."

When I arrived for the lesson, Lou's eyes twinkled. Short and muscular, with a wild crop of dark curls, he bustled around setting up his screen beside a rack of sale-priced cross-country skis. He said, with a grin, "The first thing in the lesson is that you must buy a new projector, a carousel. That is essential. The slide tray is circular and it never sticks."

Then he said, "Lesson two is, you need to write a little script for yourself and learn it. You should try to sound like a character. Tell funny little stories on yourself. By learning the script, I do not mean memorize it, just practice what you plan to say with each slide. Photographers who set their slides to music are missing a connection with their audience. People love to feel connected."

"When you've written your script and practiced it send letters to service clubs, like Lions, Rotary, and Kiwanis. They have a program every week, and their members are there every week. At each show you sell books. And make your show only 20 minutes long. Evening shows can be a little longer."

He pressed the forward button a few times on the projector. "Now tell me a story that goes with these slides."

We worked for an hour or so on what I should say, and the kinds of slides I should use. He said I needed to use sets of slides that told trip stories rather than ones that just showed places. When I showed slides of my first trip up Fourth of July Creek with the kids when we couldn't find the lake, Lou said to exaggerate what I said. "Make the rocks and ruts bigger, the snow deeper, and the kids behavior worse."

Although Wayne had just given me the Bell & Howell projector for Christmas, I bought a carousel projector with my first book earnings. I wrote a script to go with the slides, trying to make myself into the funny lady in the sunbonnet with the five wild children that Lou had suggested I be. I found my stories were funny enough without having to exaggerate. Then I wrote letters to service clubs offering a free slide show.

At first I found giving the shows as scary as giving my graduation speech in the ninth grade, but gradually I learned to enjoy the audiences, especially when they laughed.

Later I realized that by writing my book to let people know about Idaho mountains, I had carved a mark on them that is long-lasting. By drawing attention to the area I like to think my book made it more likely the White Clouds and Boulders would be named wilderness, but if so, it took 36 years. That happened at last on August 7, 2015 with an unanimous act of Congress.

After my book came out in March of 1979, I was eager to go on more hikes, but I felt I needed a reason to keep on hiking so much. At the slide shows people kept asking me for information about places I hadn't seen. So I asked Cliff if I wrote another hiking guidebook what he would like it to be on. He suggested I draw a circle around Boise and do hikes within the circle.

In early July, I took Stuart, who was then 12, on the first hike for the new book. We drove up Snowbank Mountain near Cascade and hiked to Shirts Lake, which had a sweeping view of Lake Cascade. We found only a sketchy trail to it and no sign. I thought it definitely needed to be in the book so people could find it.

As I watched Stuart fish in Shirts Lake, I thought of my grandfather Arthur Cathcart building his cabin by hand at Fallen Leaf, California, in 1912, and my great grandfather Fenimore Shepard building his summer cottage on Lake Bomoseen, Vermont, about 1895. I remembered the struggles Wayne and I and our kids went through to build our cabin in the Sawtooths in 1968 and to finish it, which took 24 years. Staying in a cabin in the mountains seemed to be vital for my family.

The landscape of the Sawtooths and White Clouds overlies the landscape of Fallen Leaf in my mind as though they are the maps for life that I have followed. Time and my choices have only deepened its lines. The feelings of joy and refuge are the same now as they were to me as a child and young adult. Although my parents and grandparents are gone now, I am thankful they passed on their love of mountains and wild places to me and helped me hand on that love to my children, grandchildren, and others. Loving mountains is still the glue that binds our family together, still the leavening that lightens our souls.

INDEX